Writing
Business Programs
in C Language

CHILTON'S BUSINESS COMPUTING SERIES

Other books by Phillip Good in CHILTON'S BUSINESS COMPUTING SERIES

Computerize Your Business
A Critic's Guide to Software for Apple and Apple-Compatible Computers
A Critic's Guide to Software for CP/M Computers
A Critic's Guide to Software for the IBM PC and PC-Compatible Computers
A Critic's Guide to Word Processing for IBM PC and PC-Compatible Computers
Increasing Your Business Effectiveness through Computer Communications
Managing Your Office with Macintosh (coauthored with Kathryn Good)

Writing
Business Programs
in C Language

Martin Franz
and
Phillip Good

CHILTON BOOK COMPANY

Radnor, Pennsylvania

Library of Congress Cataloging in Publication Data
Franz, Martin.
  Writing business programs in C language.
  (Chilton's business computing series)
  Includes index.
  1. C (Computer program language) 2. Business—Data
processing. I. Good, Phillip I. II. Title. III. Series.
HF5548.5.C12F73 1985   650.′028′5424   84–45695
ISBN 0–8019–7611–1

1 2 3 4 5 6 7 8 9 0   4 3 2 1 0 9 8 7 6 5

Contents

INTRODUCTION   **1**

1 FINANCIAL PLANNERS   **5**

Lease/Purchase Decision   6
A Better Lease/Purchase Decision   8
✓   Variable Name Rules   9
✓   Floating-Point Numbers   9
Monthly Mortgage Payment   11
✓   Operators and Expressions   12
✓   Bugstopper's Notebook   13
Mortgage Present Value—Can You Afford It?   15
Amortization Schedule   18
✓   The *for* Statement   19
What You Learned in Chapter 1   22

2 THE DESKTOP CALENDAR   **23**

Creating and Using Functions   23
✓   Function Arguments   25
✓   Declaring Function Type   26
Julian Format   27
✓   Relational Operators   29
From Julian Format   30

Test Program   31
Number of Days Between Dates   33
Day of the Week for a Date   35
✓   Integer Numbers   36
A Perpetual Calendar   38
A More Complete Calendar   42
What You Learned in Chapter 2   45

3   WORKING WITH TEXT — 46

Character Variables   46
✓   Character Data   47
Character Arrays   49
Strings   50
✓   The *printf( )* Function   52
Mailing Labels   53
Filling and Centering Text   55
The Improved Calendar   58
What You Learned in Chapter 3   61

4   AN ELECTRONIC CHECKBOOK — 63

Programming Techniques   63
Main Program   65
✓   Variable Scope   67
✓   Unsigned Numbers   68
Adding Checks   71
Listing Checks   72
Deleting Checks   74
✓   The *sscanf( )* Function   76
Changing Checks   78
✓   The *atoi( )* Function   79
✓   The *atof( )* Function   80
Reading and Writing Files   82
What You Learned in Chapter 4   86

5   BUSINESS STATISTICS — 87

A Plan for a Statistics Program   87
The *main( )* Function   90
Getting a File Name   91
Processing Statistics   93
Asking for Another   95
Sample Run: Testing Everything   95
What You Learned in Chapter 5   97

6 RECORD KEEPING   98

Pointers in C   99
✓ Pointers and Functions   101
✓ That Funny &   102
Selecting Records   103
Sorting Records   108
A Name and Phone File   113
What You Learned in Chapter 6   116

7 THE BOTTOM LINE: FORMATTING REPORTS   117

A General Report Program   117
Using Your Printer   120
Generic Report Functions   121
Printing Mailing Labels   124
✓ Bugstopper's Notebook: Using "Magic Numbers"   125
Printing a Formatted Check Register   128
A Better Check Register   131
Design Your Own Reports   136
What You Learned in Chapter 7   136

8 WRITING YOUR OWN C PROGRAMS   137

Advanced Programming Concepts   137
Interpreters   140
Compilers   142
Libraries   149
Wrapping Up   150

APPENDIX I   USING YOUR COMPILER   151

Unix Version 7 (or Xenix) C   152
Lattice C   153
Computer Innovations' C-86 C   154
Computer Innovations' Introducing C   155
Aztec C   156

**APPENDIX II   ADDITIONAL FUNCTIONS
AND PROGRAM CHANGES**   157

Additional Functions   157
Additional Program Changes   159

APPENDIX III MORE ABOUT FILES IN C 162

Additional Access Modes   162
Additional Functions   163
Redirecting I/O   164
A Word About Portability   166

APPENDIX IV STATISTICAL FUNCTIONS 167

Mean and Variance Revisited   167
Covariance and Correlation   170
Multilinear Regression   172
Rank Tests   173

APPENDIX V C PROGRAM REFRESHER 177

Before You Start   177
The *main( )* Function   177
Declaring Variables   178
Using Functions   178
Using Statements   179
Using Expressions   180
Using Constants   181
Some Important Functions   182
Subscripts and Pointers   183
Common Bug List   183

INDEX 184

Writing
Business Programs
in C Language

Introduction

Congratulations. You've just joined the more than 100,000 businesspeople who are already programming in C language. C is the first choice of software developers who write mass-market programs. Digital Research, Infocom, Mark of the Unicorn, Microsoft, and Visicorp (to name a few companies) all write and publish computer programs in C.

Why is C so popular among software developers? There are three main reasons. First, C is portable. The C language was designed to be independent of the computer it is running on. The result is that programs written in C can be run virtually unchanged on 8-bit, 16-bit, or 32-bit computers from the Apple to the VAX, whether the operating system is Apple's DOS, CP/M, MS-DOS, UNIX, or XENIX. So the programs you develop on an IBM PC today can easily be transported to an Apple][or a Macintosh tomorrow. This portability enables developers to adapt their products for the latest computer models.

Second, C lets developers bring their products to market sooner. It saves them time and cuts personnel costs. This is because a single concise statement in C can replace half a dozen statements in BASIC and even more in assembler. C's powerful statements mean fewer lines to write per program and reduced editing and debugging time. The result: reduced development and training costs and increased productivity.

Finally, C offers performance. Programs written in C run at assembly-language speed yet take only a fraction of the development time of assembly-language programs. C offers the conveniences of a high-level programming language, yet it is fast enough to do graphics, music, and data acquisition.

But C is not just for professional programmers. C is a remarkably simple programming language with fewer than 30 key words. You don't have to use features you don't need or understand. The fundamentals of C are so simple you'll be programming productively and profitably by the time you've completed the first chapter of this book. With a little practice, you can use C for all your own programming needs.

The goal of this book is to get you started programming in C quickly and profitably. Instead of rote tutorial sections, this book gives you working, easy-to-understand programs you can look at, run, and modify. These programs fulfill actual business needs; some have home and personal applications as well. They have been arranged in increasing complexity so that you won't get in over your head. By the end of this book, you'll have mastered enough of C to write your own programs and to learn the more complex features of the language as needed.

In Chapters 1–3 you develop a series of short programs that work with the three essentials of business: time, words, and money. Chapter 1 provides you with four simple programs to perform essential financial calculations. The first of these, the lease/purchase decision, will help you determine whether it is more profitable to buy a piece of equipment or to lease it. The second program computes the monthly payment for a conventional home mortgage. You can also use it to determine the monthly payout on a retirement plan or other form of annuity.

The third program in Chapter 1 is the "reverse" of the annuity program and will tell you if you can afford a mortgage. The last program builds on the previous ones to produce a mortgage amortization schedule with accumulated interest (a must for tax purposes). As you write these programs, you learn how easy it is to do input, calculations, and simple output in C.

One of the mainstays of any manager's desk is the desktop calendar. You can use the calendar programs you develop in Chapter 2 to make appointments, to check on past appointments for tax purposes, to compute the number of days until Christmas, and to reconcile delivery dates.

The calendar program is a complicated one, so we teach you how to use short, easy-to-write functions to assemble larger programs. Functions are important to C programmers since they help organize computer programs for better maintenance and enhancement. In addition, once written and tested, functions can be used repeatedly in different programs. You'll be able to use the calendar and other functions you develop in this book in many of your own C programs later.

Words are a mainstay of any business, and in Chapter 3 you learn how to manipulate names and addresses through character variables, arrays, and strings. You learn how to display mailing labels and to center and emphasize text.

In Chapters 4–8, you apply what you've learned to the development of larger, general-purpose programs. The first such program, presented in Chapter 4, is an electronic checkbook. With it, you'll be able to enter, change, and delete checks and deposits as well as list the transactions on file. In later chapters, you extend and modify this checkbook program so that you can find and sort checks, print a check register, and compute the "float."

To help you successfully write and test such a large program, you learn several additional techniques of program design in Chapter 4, including "left-corner" construction, a technique that resolves any programming task into small, easily tested pieces. With these techniques you can now approach almost any programming task.

The checkbook program you write in Chapter 4 is so general that you can use it for many different record-keeping jobs. In Chapter 5, you write a program that processes files created by the checkbook program and computes essential statistics, including the number of items in the file and their total, mean, and maximum. The functions you develop can be applied to any set of numeric data for which statistics are required.

In Chapter 6 you add selection and sort functions to your checkbook program. You can use these functions to select lists of prime prospects, check on orders, and print out your mailing list in zip code order. With the improved "little database" program, you build a "Rolodex" file of employee names, phone numbers, and departments. You can use this improved program to help you keep a "to do" list, track business expenses for accounting purposes, organize your phone bill, or keep an inventory of home or office equipment for insurance purposes.

Of course, there's no advantage to having a computer system unless you can produce reports you can show to your boss, your colleagues, your CPA, and your banker. Accurate, useful reports are the most important part of any business software system. In Chapter 7, you learn how to format your printed reports to meet a variety of business needs and create report "modules" for use with your new, improved checkbook program.

In Chapter 7, you write a program to create mailing labels from a name and address file. You also write a program to print a check register that shows the check number, the amount, the date written, the date cashed, and a description of the check. You add a running balance, and then as a bonus for completing all your fundamental C programming requirements, you program a float calculation that may save you a hundred dollars or more each year.

By Chapter 8, you are ready to write your own programs. Chapter 8 describes several features of C programming that you can use to great advantage when developing your own applications software. It also describes the popular C interpreters and compilers and how to choose among them.

Appendix I, Using Your Compiler, and Appendix II, Additional Functions and Program Changes, specify how to use your particular compiler to run the programs listed in this book. They cover these compilers: Unix Version 7 C, Xenix C, Lattice C, Computer Innovations' C-86 C and Introducing C, and Aztec C.

The benefits that come to you from using this book are many and long lasting. First, you learn the fundamentals of C programming, calculations, character manipulation, and file management—everything you need to develop programs of your own. Second, you build a library of applications software written in C, including financial management programs, a desktop calendar, and an electronic checkbook. Last, but most important, you receive an extensive library of functions for text, time, and money management, the functions that are the fundamental building blocks of C and the foundation of all business programming.

Congratulations. Not only does this book get you started programming in C quickly, but it also provides you with tools that you can apply profitably for a long time.

Financial Planners
1

This chapter provides you with four simple programs to perform essential financial calculations. The first, the lease/purchase decision, presents the basics of C program structure and contains a few of the "workhorse" functions you'll be using frequently. The second program calculates the monthly payment for a conventional home mortgage (or the monthly pay-out on a retirement plan or other annuity). You learn how easy it is to do input, calculations, and simple output in C.

The third program is the reverse of the second. It computes a mortgage's present value given the size of the payments you want to make and the amount of interest you have to pay. The last program in this chapter produces a mortgage amortization schedule with accumulated interest, principle equity, and so forth. This program introduces you to C's *for* and *if* statements, which let you do repeated calculations with one or two simple commands.

When you type in the programs in this chapter, be sure to key in the comments as well. A comment in a C program is any text enclosed in /* */, for example:

```
/* Listing 1-1. Lease/Purchase Decision */
```

Comments are indispensable when you need to refer back to a program after a lapse of time. Remember to use lots of comments in your own programs, too.

The programs presented in this chapter use several C functions. For now, you only need to know that a function is a small piece of a C program, a piece you can often use in several different programs. Some C compilers and interpreters require you to convert or enter the functions you need; refer to Appendix II for information on this.

(By typing in the listings for the functions used in this chapter, you will be building up a library of functions that will prove invaluable time-savers when you sit down to write your own programs in the future.)

LEASE/PURCHASE DECISION

DESCRIPTION

This program calculates the payback period on a lease. The payback period, in months, is the number of monthly payments you need to make to equal the price that would have been charged had the piece of equipment been purchased outright. With this figure in hand, the decision to buy or lease can be based on how long you expect the useful life of the equipment to be. (If you're in the leasing business, you may want to print out a copy of the results for each of your prospective customers.) This program demonstrates the basic structure of all C programs, as you'll see in the next section.

HOW IT WORKS

The leasing program consists of a single function, called *main()*. Every C program you write must have a main function. The structure of a simple C program looks like this:

```
/*
     Comments that tell what the program does
*/

main()
{
     statements that name and describe the variables;

     statements that make up the program;
}
```

Note that squiggly brackets, called braces, enclose statements that describe the variables and the statements that make up the program.

Franz & Good: Writing Business Programs in C Language (Chilton)

FINANCIAL PLANNERS

When writing programs in C, you must have a closing brace for each opening brace.

BEFORE YOU START

Are you ready to begin entering your first program? You'll need to refer to the instructions that came with your C compiler or interpreter. You may be able to enter the listing by using the same word processor you use to write letters (see Appendix I).

Whatever C compiler or interpreter you use, you'll find that several casual readings of the manual are preferable to one intensive reading, at least to start. Because the programs in this book are graded in complexity, you won't need to be familiar with the advanced features of your compiler until the final chapter. To be on the safe side, also read through those sections of Appendix I and II that apply to your C compiler.

LISTING

```
/* Listing 1-1. Lease/Purchase Decision */

main()
{
        float lamount, pprice;

        lamount = gf();
        pprice = gf();
        printf("%7.2f\n", pprice/lamount);
}
```

SAMPLE RUN

```
? 100
? 2000
20.00
```

NOTES

For this program, the *main()* function is very simple. The first statement of the function names the variables the program uses. This statement is called a *declaration*. The statement

```
float lamount, pprice;
```

declares that the variables named *lamount* and *pprice* will contain floating-point decimal numbers (e.g., 12.98 as opposed to the integer 12). (Note that this statement, like all statements in C, ends with a semicolon.) You don't need to worry about how the numbers are stored in the computer's memory or how big they are. The C language takes care of this for you.

The next line in the program

```
lamount = gf();
```

reads in the lease amount that you have entered at the keyboard using the function *gf()* and stores it in the variable *lamount*. [The function *gf()*, similar to INPUT in BASIC, outputs a question mark.]

The third line reads the purchase price into the variable *pprice*, again using the function *gf()*. These two statements are similar to the INPUT statement in BASIC. As each statement is executed, the computer stops, waits for input, and then stores the number you enter in the indicated variable.

Finally, the last line in the program prints the payback in months. The single statement

```
printf("%7.2f\n", pprice/lamount);
```

divides the purchase price by lease amount and prints the result. [The *printf()* function is used exactly like the PRINT statement in BASIC.] The text enclosed in quotation marks is called a *format*, and you'll learn more about how it works in later chapters. For now, note that the statement shown is similar to PRINT PPRICE/LAMOUNT in BASIC.

A BETTER LEASE/PURCHASE DECISION

DESCRIPTION

You've probably noticed that the preceding program doesn't do a very good job of telling you about the input it needs. Such brief programs, while useful for learning, are not very convenient to work with on a daily basis. The new version of the lease/purchase decision program listed below is easier to use because it prompts for each value that must be supplied. The new version also converts the payback period from months to years for easier reading.

Variable Name Rules

1. Variable names in C are made up of letters, digits, or an underscore character, for example: amount _1.

2. The name can have any number of characters, though only the first eight are used to distinguish a variable name.

3. Traditional C style is to have variable names in lowercase characters.

4. The name and type of the variable must be declared before it can be used in a statement.

Floating-Point Numbers

Floating-point numbers usually occupy four bytes of memory. This allows six- or seven-digit precision and a range of 10^{-38} to 10^{38}.

A floating-point constant in a C program is any sequence of digits that includes a decimal point or an exponent, such as the numbers

$$10.0 \quad .203 \quad 1. \quad 1.0e10 \quad -8.25e-3.$$

HOW IT WORKS

In this program, an extra variable called *payback* has been added to hold the payback period in months. Also, additional statements have been added to prompt for the input required and better document the program's operation. The statements

```
printf("\n\nLease/Purchase Decision\n");

printf("\nWhat is the monthly rent");

printf("What is the outright purchase price");
```

simply print the text enclosed in quotation marks. You saw a similar print statement in the preceding listing. Only the two-character combination \n needs explanation: Whenever C encounters this combination of characters, called *newline*, a return and linefeed are sent to the display screen. Before the text is printed, the display skips to the next line of output on the screen.

This program uses a new function, *dashes(23)*, which prints a string of 23 dashes on the screen. The function *(25)* would print 25 dashes, and so forth. The line of dashes underlines and sets off the title of the program when it is executed. We will use the *dashes()* function in many other programs in this book to underline titles and headings and set off tables.

LISTING

```
/* Listing 1-2. A Better Lease/Purchase Decision
   Asks for monthly lease amount and purchase cost, then computes
   payback in months and years
*/

main()
{
        float lamount, payback, pprice;

        printf("\n\nLease/Purchase Decision\n");
        dashes(23);

        printf("\nWhat is the monthly rent");
        lamount = gf();
```

```
        printf ("What is the outright purchase price");
        pprice = gf();

        payback = pprice/lamount;
        printf("\nThe lease will pay back in %3.2f months, or ",
            payback);
        printf("%3.2f years.\n", payback/12.0);
}
```

SAMPLE RUN

```
Lease/Purchase Decision
----------------------


What is the monthly rent? 100
What is the outright purchase price? 2000

The lease will pay back in 20.00 months, or 1.67 years.
```

NOTES

You may do calculations inside a *printf()* statement, as in

```
printf("%3.2f years.\n", payback/12.0);
```

where the conversion from months to years is accomplished by dividing by 12.

MONTHLY MORTGAGE PAYMENT

DESCRIPTION

This program calculates the monthly payment on a mortgage loan. This type of loan is called an annuity because the payments are made periodically, usually every month. To use the program, you must input the following information:

k   the number of years on the mortgage

i   the annual interest rate

pv   the value of the mortgage

√

Operators and Expressions

You do arithmetic in C with:

+   addition

−   subtraction

*   multiplication

/   division

%   remainder

In complex expressions, * and / are performed before + and −. You can rearrange the order of these operations however you wish by using ( ).

Bugstopper's Notebook

Are you having problems getting these programs to run the first time? The most frequent errors are

1. Failing to put a semicolon (;) at the end of each statement

2. Misspellings (if you listed the variable *pprice* in a declaration, the program won't recognize *price* unless you've declared this name separately)

3. Having an unmatched parenthesis or brace

Check these sources of error each time you enter a new listing.

The program then calculates the value of the monthly payment (pmt) using the formula:

$$pmt = pv * i / (1 - (1 + i)^{-k})$$

HOW IT WORKS

The program uses both the *dashes()* and *gf()* functions mentioned earlier. The values for *pv*, *k*, and *i* are entered, and *k* and *i* are converted to the number of months and monthly interest, respectively.

A new function, *pow()*, is used in calculating *pmt* according to the formula shown above. The *pow()* function returns the value of its first variable (argument) raised to the power of the second. That is, pow(2, 3) returns the answer 2*2*2 or 8. (Quick: What is pow(10, 6)? The answer is 1 million.)

Not all compilers have a *pow()* function, or it may be called by a different name. Check Appendix II for instructions on modifying the listing below to meet your requirements.

LISTING

```
/* Listing 1-3. Compute Mortgage (Annuity) Payment

   You input these variables:

        i         periodic interest rate (input as APR)
        k         number of payments (input as number of years)
        pv        present value (value of mortgage)

   The program calculates:

        pmt       the monthly payment
*/

main()
{
        float i, k, pv, pmt;
        float w1, w2;

        printf("\nMonthly Mortgage Payment\n");
        dashes(24);
```

```
printf("\nWhat is the value of the mortgage (pv)");
pv = gf();

printf("\nHow many years is the mortgage for (k)");
k = gf();
k = k * 12.0;
printf("That is %4.1f monthly payments.\n", k);

printf("\nWhat is the annual interest rate (i)");
i = gf();
i = (i/12.0) / 100.0;
printf("That is a monthly interest rate of %6.4f.\n", i);

/* calculate the payment amount */
w1 = (1 + i); w2 = -k;
pmt = pv * (i / (1 - pow(w1, w2)));
printf("\nThe monthly payment amount is %7.2f.\n", pmt);
}
```

SAMPLE RUN

```
Monthly Mortgage Payment
------------------------


What is the value of the mortgage (pv)? 3000

How many years is the mortgage for (k)? 3
That is 36.0 monthly payments.

What is the annual interest rate (i)? 9.5
That is a monthly interest rate of 0.0079.

The monthly payment amount is 96.10.
```

MORTGAGE PRESENT VALUE—CAN YOU AFFORD IT?

DESCRIPTION

This program is the "reverse" of the Monthly Mortgage Payment program. Given an interest rate, the number of years, and the monthly payment you want to make, this program computes the present value of the mortgage you can afford. (It doesn't, of course, take into account taxes and processing charges.)

The formula used to calculate the present value is:

$$pv = pmt * ((1 - (1 + i)^{-k}) / i)$$

HOW IT WORKS

Inspection of the listing shown below reveals that this program is very similar to the Monthly Mortgage Payment program presented in the last section. In fact, if you use a text editor, you can create the Present Value program by making just a few modifications to statements in the Monthly Mortgage Payment program. (*Hint:* This is the way most programming professionals do it. Copying and modifying old programs cuts down on the number of typing errors and the time you spend correcting them. Just remember to give the new program a different file name, or you'll over-write and destroy the old version of the program.)

LISTING

```
/* Listing 1-4. Compute Mortgage (Annuity) Present Value

    You input these variables:
        i           periodic interest rate (input as APR)
        k           number of payments (input as number of years)
        pmt         monthly payment amount

    The program calculates:

        pv          the amount of the mortgage you can afford
*/

main()
{
        float i, k, pv, pmt;
        float w1, w2;

        printf("\nMortgage Present Value\n");
        dashes(22);
```

Franz & Good: Writing Business Programs in C Language (Chilton)

FINANCIAL PLANNERS

```
printf("\nWhat is the monthly payment (pmt)");
pmt = gf();

printf("\nHow many years is the mortgage for (k)");
k = gf();
k = k * 12.0;
printf("That is %4.1f monthly payments.\n", k);

printf("\nWhat is the annual interest rate (i)");
i = gf();
i = (i/12.0) / 100.0;
printf("That is a monthly interest rate of %6.4f.\n", i);

/* calculate the payment amount */
w1 = (1 + i); w2 = -k;
pv = pmt * ((1 - pow(w1, w2)) / i);
printf("\nThe present value you can afford is %7.2f.\n", pv);
{
```

SAMPLE RUN

```
Mortgage Present Value
----------------------


What is the monthly payment (pmt)? 96.10

How many years is the mortgage for (k)? 3
That is 36.0 monthly payments.

What is the annual interest rate (i)? 9.5
That is a monthly interest rate of 0.0079.

The present value you can afford is 3000.00.
```

NOTES

Test this program using the same monthly payment, interest rate, and number of years as the Monthly Mortgage Payment program. You should get the same present value. This use of a test case or benchmark problem is one example of good programming practice. Be sure to use test cases as you begin writing programs of your own.

AMORTIZATION SCHEDULE

DESCRIPTION

Using the formulas and program structure of the last two programs, the Amortization Schedule program computes and prints an amortization schedule for a mortgage. An amortization schedule tells, for any period, the balance remaining on the mortgage and the cumulative interest paid. The formula used for the balance remaining after m months is:

bal = pv * (w[m] − w[k]/(w[m] * (1 − w[k])))

where w[m] = (1 + i) − m.

Cumulative interest is total payments less owner's equity, or:

intr = m * pmt − (pv − bal)

To use this program, you input k, i, and pv as you did in the previous programs. The program will then print a table that shows the period, payment, balance remaining, and cumulative interest on the mortgage.

HOW IT WORKS

Until now, the programs you've entered have been strictly "calculator" type. You typed in values for the variables and out came the answer. With this new program, you take advantage of the computer's and C's ability to do repeated calculations.

When you examine the listing below, you may not find many differences between this program and the Mortgage Present Value program presented earlier. There are only minor differences, for example, in the variable declarations and the statements following the entry of the annual interest rate.

Here, the program listing begins to get interesting. The program includes a *for* statement that will calculate the balance and accumulated interest for every period, one after the other, until the mortgage is paid off. The general format of a *for* statement in C is:

```
for (initial statement; test; increment statement) {
     statements that make up the loop;
}
```

√

The *for* Statement

The *for* statement has the format:

      for (initialize; test; increment) any C statement;

In English, this looks like:

      initialize
      while test is true
            any C statement
            increment
      repeat the loop

The initialize, test, and increment statements can be anything you wish, but they usually control a single variable.

In theory, the *for* loop is similar to FOR . . . NEXT loops in BASIC or DO loops in FORTRAN. In practice, however, the *for* loop is much more general, since the initial statement, test, and increment statement can be any other C statement. You'll learn more about the *for* statement in upcoming chapters. For now, just make sure you get the placement of the braces and semicolons correct.

LISTING

```
/* Listing 1-5.  Compute Mortgage Amortization Schedule

    You input these variables:

        i        periodic interest rate (input as APR)
        k        number of payments (input as number of years)
        pv       the amount of the mortgage you can afford

    The program calculates:

        pmt      monthly payment amount
        bal      the balance at the end of the current period
        intr     the cumulative interest paid
*/

main()
{
        float bal, i, intr, k, m, pv, pmt;
        float w1, w2, w3, w4;

        printf("\nMortgage Amortization Schedule\n");
        dashes(30);

        printf("\nHow many years is the mortgage for (k)");
        k = gf();
        k = k * 12.0;
        printf("That is %4.1f monthly payments.\n", k);

        printf("\nWhat is the annual interest rate (i)");
        i = gf();
        i = (i/12.0) / 100.0;
        printf("That is a monthly interest rate of %6.4f.\n", i);
```

```
        printf("\nWhat is the value of the mortgage (pv)");
        pv = gf();

        w1 = (1 + i); w2 = -k; w3 = pow (w1,w2);
        pmt = pv * i /(1 - w3);
        printf("\nThe monthly payment amount is %7.2f.\n", pmt);
        printf("\nMonth    Payment    Balance    Interest\n");
        dashes(37);

        printf("\n");
        for (m = 1; m<k+1; m++) {
                w2 = -m; w4 = pow(w1, w2);
                bal = (pv/ w4) * (w4-w3)/(1-w3);
                intr = m * pmt - pv + bal;
        printf("%4.0f    %7.2f    %7.2f    %7.2f\n", m, pmt, bal, intr);
        }
}
```

SAMPLE RUN

```
Mortgage Amortization Schedule
------------------------------

How many years is the mortgage for (k)? 3
That is 36.0 monthly payments.

What is the annual interest rate (i)? 9.5
That is a monthly interest rate of 0.0079.

What is the value of the mortgage (pv)? 3000
The monthly payment amount is 96.10.
```

Month	Payment	Balance	Interest
1	96.10	2927.65	23.75
2	96.10	2854.73	46.93
-			
-			
36	96.10	0.00	459.55

NOTES

Yes, the accumulated interest will be a very large number relative to the present value of the mortgage. This is not necessarily a bug in the program, just in the economy.

Note that the *printf()* statement inside the *for* loop outputs a list of variables instead of just one value. As a result, you will often use the *printf()* function to output the results of your programs. In a later chapter you'll learn more about the *printf()* function and the myriad of formatting options it supports.

WHAT YOU LEARNED IN CHAPTER 1

In this chapter, you've used five sample C programs of increasing complexity. By now you will have noticed that each new program borrows statements from previous ones. The time-saving advantage of C comes from such borrowing, which minimizes the need to type and retype statements. In the next chapter you learn how to convert parts of your program into functions to facilitate their repeated use.

Here's a summary of the statements you've learned in this chapter:

float	declares floating-point variable
for	looping statement

And here's a list of the functions you've seen so far:

main()	main function of program
dashes()	prints dashes to highlight text
gf()	gets floating-point number
printf()	prints text and variables
pow()	power function

The Desktop Calendar

2

One of the mainstays of any manager's desk is the desktop calendar. You use it to make appointments, to check on past appointments for tax purposes, to compute the number of days until Christmas, and to reconcile delivery dates. In this chapter, you will develop a perpetual calendar program for office use good through the year 2100.

This program is a complicated one, so like most professional programmers, we've adopted a step-by-step approach, developing the program a piece at a time and then combining the pieces. In C, these individual pieces of a program are called *functions*. Functions are important in programming because they help organize your computer programs for better maintenance and enhancement. Once written and tested, functions can also be used repeatedly in a variety of different programs. You will find many uses for the calendar functions developed in this chapter in other C programs you write.

CREATING AND USING FUNCTIONS

A function is a set of program statements that defines a complete calculation or procedure. When you use the name of a function in your program, this calculation or procedure is performed as if the statements that make up the procedure were written into the program at that point. In operation, C functions are similar to procedures in Pascal or subroutines in FORTRAN.

There are two steps to using a function. The first step is to create and define it. When you define a function you identify the name of the function and the names of the variables (arguments) that will be passed to it by the program or function that invokes it. A function definition looks like this:

```
function name(arguments)
argument declaration statements;
{
    variable declaration statements;
    statements used in the function;
}
```

The declaration statements for the external variables or arguments are similar to the declaration statements for internal variables that you used in the last chapter. For example, in the definition of the function *julmdy()*, below, we write:

```
float julmdy(m, d, y)
float m, d, y;
{
    float jul, m1, y1;
}
```

Note in this example (and in the listing below) how the arguments *m, d, y* are used for passing information between the function and the program that invoked it, while the variables *jul, m1, y1* are used for calculations within the function.

After a function has been defined, it can then be *called*. To call a function, you place a statement in the calling program with the name of the function and a list of the variables you wish to use with it. Examples of function-calling statements used in the last chapter include:

```
dashes(23);

pprice = gf();

printf("Lease/Purchase Decision\n");
```

Franz & Good: Writing Business Programs in C Language (Chilton)

THE DESKTOP CALENDAR

V

Function Arguments

When a function is called, the arguments passed to it are assigned to the variables declared in the function definition (header), left to right for as many arguments as you pass. For example, if

$$x = func(2, 3, 4);$$

and

```
func(a, b, c)
float a, b, c;
{
```

Then $a = 2$, $b = 3$, and $c = 4$ inside *func()*.

C will not tell you if you have passed the wrong number or type of arguments to a function. The function will simply return an incorrect result. It's easy to make this mistake when writing programs, so be alert for it.

√

Declaring Function Type

Like other variables, the result a function returns must be declared as *float, char,* etc. This can be done in the function's header:

> float func(a, b, c)
> float a, b, c;

or in the function that uses the result:

> float func();

Notice the empty (). This tells C that the function named *func* is to be considered a floating-point variable.

If not declared anywhere, a function is assumed to return an *int* (integer) value. If it is not used in an expression, this *int* is discarded.

Note that the arguments of a function can be constants like 23, variables like *pprice*, or even the results of a calculation like 2 * x + b. The value each argument takes can be different each time the function is called.

Functions may be called from any point in a program, even from inside other functions. In most cases, you will want to define a function whenever there is a set of calculations that will be used repeatedly or in several programs. In the next section, we define two functions that you will use repeatedly for converting dates in and out of Julian format.

JULIAN FORMAT

DESCRIPTION

In this section you develop a series of functions that are essential for almost all calculations involving dates and durations. The first function, *julmdy()*, converts a date such as 09/03/86 to a numeric or Julian format. The numeric format allows you to perform arithmetic on dates by simple addition or subtraction. You won't need to keep a calendar always at hand. ("Thirty days has. . . . Or is it just during a leap year?")

The remaining functions *mjul()*, *djul()*, and *yjul()* convert back from the Julian format to months, days, and years. By converting to a Julian format at the beginning of a program and back to a conventional format at the end, you can eliminate many unnecessary intermediate calculations. (Don't believe us? Quick, how many days between December 18, 1983, and March 1, 1985?)

The Julian date is the number of days since January 1, 4713 B.C. (although other reference dates may be used). We can compute an interval between two Julian dates by simple subtraction, rather than by counting on our fingers.

LISTING

```
/* Listing 2-1. julmdy() Converts Date to Julian Day Number */

float julmdy(m, d, y)
float m, d, y;
{
        float jul, m1, y1;
```

```
        if (m > 2) {
                m1 = m + 1;
                y1 = y;
        }
        else {
                m1 = m + 13;
                y1 = y - 1;
        }
        jul = floor(365.25 * y1) + floor(30.6001 * m1) + d +
                1720982;
        return jul;
}
```

HOW IT WORKS

In the function above, you see two new types of C statements. The first
type is called the *compound statement*. In C, several simple statements
can be enclosed by braces so that they can be treated as one single statement by *if* and *for*. With the compound statement, you can group several
statements together and have them computed as a unit. The general format of a compound statement is:

```
    {
        one or more C statements;
    }
```

In the compound statement following if (m > 2)

```
{
    m1 = m + 1;
    y1 = y;
}
```

Both the simple statements contained inside the braces are executed if m
> 2.

The other statement new to you is the *else* statement. An *else* spec-
ifies a statement to be executed if the condition in a matching *if* statement
is false. An *else* must always be paired with an *if* statement. The format
of an *if* and a matching *else* in C is:

Franz & Good: Writing Business Programs in C Language (Chilton)

Relational Operators

In an *if, for,* or *while* statement, you can use the following relational operators to compare two variables or constants:

= =	equal
! =	not equal
<	less than
>	greater than
<=	less than or equal
>=	greater than or equal

You can also combine two or more relational expressions with the following:

&&	both expressions must be true (logical and)
||	neither expression can be false (logical or)

```
if (condition)
    statement executed if true;
else
    statement executed if false;
```

In the Julian conversion function above, we are forced to use an *if-else* sequence because of the need to correct for leap years. To simplify these corrections, we treat January and February in the program as if they were in the previous year. The *if* and *else* statements are used to distinguish between the case when a day falls in March or later (m > 3) or when it falls in these two months (else m = 1 and m = 2).

Our conversion function uses a second function called *floor()*. (As we remarked above, a function can call a function can call another function and so on almost indefinitely.) The *floor()* function returns the largest integer less than the value of the argument passed to it. For example, floor(2.5) returns 2.0 as its result. You may need to add the *floor()* listing as described in Appendix II.

FROM JULIAN FORMAT

The next functions we need for our perpetual calendar program convert from the Julian format to months, days, and years. The variables *m*, *d*, and *y* have the same meaning as in the preceeding example, and again the *floor()* function is used repeatedly.

LISTING

```
/* Listing 2-2. Convert Julian Day Number to Date */

float djul(jul)
float jul;
{
    float dayno, m, d, y;

    dayno = jul - 1720982;
    y = floor((dayno - 122.1)/365.25);
    m = floor((dayno - floor(365.25 * y))/30.6001);
    d = dayno - floor(365.25 * y) - floor(30.6001 * m);
    return d;
}
```

Franz & Good: Writing Business Programs in C Language (Chilton)

THE DESKTOP CALENDAR

```
float mjul(jul)
float jul;
{
        float dayno, m, d, y;

        dayno = jul - 1720982;
        y = floor((dayno - 122.1)/365.25);
        m = floor((dayno - floor(365.25 * y))/30.6001);
        if (m < 14) m = m - 1;
        else m = m - 13;
        return m;
}

float yjul(jul)
float jul;
{
        float dayno, m, d, y;

        dayno = jul - 1720982;
        y = floor((dayno - 122.1)/365.25);
        m = floor((dayno - floor(365.25 * y))/30.6001);
        if (m < 14) m = m - 1;
        else m = m - 13;
        if (m < 3) y = y + 1;
        return y;
}
```

Note the use of a nested function call in the statement

```
m = floor((dayno - floor(365.25 * y))/30.6001);
```


TEST PROGRAM

Experienced programmers never leave anything to chance. We advised
you earlier to test each of your programs before you put them into daily
use. The next listing is of a simple *main()* program to test the functions
julmdy(), *mjul()*, *djul()*, and *yjul()*. This test program converts the date
December 7, 1941, into a Julian date and then converts the Julian date
back to December 7, 1941.

LISTING

```
/* Listing 2-3. Test Julian Date Functions */

main()
{
        float jul, m, d, y;

        m = 12; d = 7; y = 1941;
        jul = julmdy(m, d, y);
        printf("%10.0f %2.0f %2.0f %0f\n", jul, m, d, y);
        m = mjul(jul);
        d = djul(jul);
        y = yjul(jul);
        printf("%10.0f %2.0f %2.0f %0f\n", jul, m, d, y);
}
```

SAMPLE RUN

```
2430336 12 7 1941
2430336 12 7 1941
```

NOTES

The output from the test says that the date December 7, 1941, is Julian day number 2,430,336 and that the reverse conversion was performed correctly as well. The *main()* function used to perform the test is an example of a *scaffold*, a simple routine written only to test other functions. The output formatting and prompting in *main()* is at a minimum to save time, since the *main()* will never be used in a "real" program, only to test the *julmdy(), mjul(), djul(),* and *yjul()* functions.

Note that several levels of indentations (tabs) are used in the listings. To make reading your own programs easier, it's a good idea to indent each compound statement. There's no law requiring you to do so—you can have any number of blanks and tabs in your C programs—but a consistent style of indenting makes your programs much easier to understand and to correct.

NUMBER OF DAYS BETWEEN DATES

DESCRIPTION

This next program uses the functions you have just defined to compute the interval between two dates. You can use this new program to compute aging dates for your accounts receivable and deadlines for your projects.

HOW IT WORKS

After you type in the date, the program converts it to the variables m, d, and y, and then to the Julian date (*jul1* or *jul2*). The Julian dates are subtracted from each other and the result is stored in the variable *diff*. An obvious complication arises if the second date comes before the first one. Can you guess how we handled it?

LISTING

```
/* Listing 2-4. Number of Days Between Two Dates */

main()
{
        float m1, d1, y1, m, d, y, jul1, jul2, diff;

        printf("Number of Days Between Two Dates\n");
        dashes(32);

        printf("\nEnter the first date\n");
        printf(" What is the month (1-12)");
        m1 = gf();
        printf(" What is the day (1-31)");
        d1 = gf();
        printf(" What is the year");
        y1 = gf();
        jul1 = julmdy(m1, d1, y1);

        printf("\nEnter the second date\n");
        printf(" What is the month (1-12)");
        m = gf();
        printf(" What is the day (1-31)");
        d = gf();
        printf(" What is the year");
        y = gf();
        jul2 = julmdy(m, d, y);
```

Franz & Good: Writing Business Programs in C Language (Chilton)

```
        diff = jul2 - jul1;
        if (diff < 0)
                printf("\nThat is %4.0f days before", -diff);
        else
                printf("\nThat is %4.0f days after", diff);
        printf("%2.0f/%2.0f/%2.0f.\n", m1, d1, 1900-y1);
}
```

SAMPLE RUN

```
Number of Days Between Two Dates
--------------------------------

Enter the first date
  What is the month (1-12)? 12
  What is the day (1-31)? 7
  What is the year? 1941

Enter the second date
  What is the month (1-12)? 12
  What is the day (1-31)? 7
  What is the year? 1942

That is 365 days after 12/ 7/41.
```

NOTES

Do you notice that the C program above consists almost entirely of calls to functions including *printf()*, *dashes()*, *mjul()*, and *julmdy()*?

We solved the program of negative durations by using a series of statements of the form:

    if (>0) { . . }
    else { . . . }

Note that you may nest several *if-else* statements inside one another providing each is set off with braces.

Franz & Good: Writing Business Programs in C Language (Chilton)

THE DESKTOP CALENDAR

DAY OF THE WEEK FOR A DATE

DESCRIPTION

This program tells the day of the week a particular calendar date falls on. You supply a date and it computes the day of the week from the Julian date.

This program introduces a new C statement, called *switch-case.* This statement has the format:

```
switch (variable) {

case constant1:
    statements executed if variable = constant1
    break;

case constant2:
    statements executed if variable = constant2
    break;

}
```

This statement is similar in concept to ON . . . GOTO in BASIC. That is, a variable called the *switch* is compared in turn with a series of constant values, called *cases.* When the switch matches the case, the statements listed under the case are executed. The entire series of case statements is enclosed between braces. You can list as many cases as you want.

This program also introduces a new variable type, *int.* An *int* is an integer variable that holds values such as 0, 1, and 2. It is used for loop counters, switches, program flags, and the like. Integers are processed faster than floating-point variables and usually (though not always) take up less space in memory. For the *switch-case* statement in this program, an *int* version of the day number, the variable *day,* is used.

HOW IT WORKS

The program uses the equations:

day # = Julian date − 1,720,982

day of week = 7 * fractional part[(day # + 5)/7]

√

Integer Numbers

Integer numbers in C usually occupy two bytes of memory. This allows a range of −32768 to 32767.

An integer constant in C is a sequence of digits with or without a sign. Here are some examples:

$$1 \quad -1 \quad 265 \quad -382 \quad 0$$

After the day of the week is computed as a number from 1 to 7, a *switch-case* statement converts it to a name (Sunday to Saturday).

LISTING

```
/* Listing 2-5. Calculate Day of the Week for a Date */

main()
{
        char date1[80];
        int day;
        float dayno, dow;
        float m, d, y, jul1;

        printf("Day of the Week for a Date\n");
        dashes(26);

        printf("\nEnter the date\n");
        printf("  What is the month (1-12)");
        m = gf();
        printf("  What is the day (1-31)");
        d = gf();
        printf("  What is the year");
        y = gf();
        jul1 = julmdy(m, d, y);

        dayno = jul1 - 1720982;
        dow = (dayno+5)/7;
        dow = 7*(dow - floor(dow));
        day = dow + 0.5;

        printf("That date falls on a ");
        switch (day) {

        case 1: printf("Monday.\n");
                break;

        case 2: printf("Tuesday.\n");
                break;

        case 3: printf("Wednesday.\n");
                break;
```

```
            case 4: printf("Thursday.\n");
                    break;

            case 5: printf("Friday.\n");
                    break;

            case 6: printf("Saturday.\n");
                    break;

            case 0: printf("Sunday.\n");
                    break;
            }
}
```

SAMPLE RUN

```
Day of the Week for a Date
--------------------------

Enter the date
  What is the month (1-12)? 12
  What is the day (1-31)? 7
  What is the year? 1941
That date falls on a Sunday.
```

A PERPETUAL CALENDAR

DESCRIPTION

This program uses the functions developed in the previous sections to make a perpetual calendar. You supply the month and the year and the program generates the calendar for it.

There is a new statement in this program, the *while* statement. This statement has the format:

while (condition)
    statement executed while condition true;

Like the *for* statement, the *while* statement is a program loop. The *while* statement relies on statements within the loop to cause the loop to terminate, and unlike the *for* loop, there is no guarantee a while loop will terminate! A "normal" termination or exit from the *while* loop occurs when the condition becomes false. (You should have checked over your program to be sure this will happen.) Another way to exit a *while* loop is with a *break* statement. The format of a *break* statement is simply

```
break;
```

When the *break* statement is encountered within a loop during execution, the program immediately exits from the loop. A *break* statement is often used in conjunction with *switch-case*.

HOW IT WORKS

First, the program asks the user for the month and the year for which a calendar is desired. Next, the program prints the heading for the calendar. The *for* statement in the program skips over the days in the first week that are in the previous month. The *while* statement computes a series of Julian dates, checking each to see if it is still in the same month. If so, the day of the month is computed and printed and another turn through the loop is made. The program terminates when the calendar is complete.

The *while* statement and the compound statement it controls are described below in English:

```
while (still in current month) {
        compute current day of the week
        if it's Saturday print a new line
        compute the day of the month
        print it
        go to the next Julian day
}
```

LISTING

```
/* Listing 2-6. Perpetual Calendar Version 1 */

main()
{
        int day, i;
        float m, m1, d, y, jul;
```

```
            printf("Perpetual Calendar\n");
            dashes(17);

            printf("\nWhat month? ");
            m = gf();
            printf("What year do you want the calendar for? ");
            y = gf();

            printf(" Su M Tu W Th F Sa\n");
            dashes(21);

            d = 1;
            m1 = m;
            jul = julmdy(m, d, y);
            day = dow(jul);

            for (i = 0; i < day; i++)
                    printf("   ");

            while (m1 == m) {
                    printf(" %2.0f", d);
                    if (day == 6) printf("\n");
                    jul = jul + 1;
                    m1 = mjul(jul);
                    day = dow(jul);
            }
            printf("\n");
}


/* return the day of the week */

dow(jul)
float jul;
{
        int day;
        float dayno, dw;

        dayno = jul - 1720982;
        dw = (dayno + 5)/7;
        day = 7*(dw - floor(dw)) + 0.5;
        return day;
}
```

NOTES

We make use of the increment operator ++ in the statement

```
i++;
```

it's as if you've written

```
i = i + 1;
```

This only works on integer variables, however; increment is not allowed on floating-point variables in some compilers. The other statements in the preceding listing are familiar until we come to the *for* loop:

```
for (i = 0; i < day; i++)

        printf("    ");
```

This statement says that we are to set *i* to the value 0 initially. Thereafter, for as long as $i <$ day, we are to increment *i* by 1 (i++) and print three blanks ("   ").

Because the program computes the day of the week in two places, we have grouped the statements that do these computations in a separate function that we call *dow()*. The listing for this new function is placed at the end of the listing for the main program. It has the same structure as other functions we have written except for the return statement that ends its listing:

```
return day;
```

Recall that in the main program we wrote the statement

```
day = dow(jul);
```

When this statement is executed, the function *dow()* is called. It processes the Julian date passed to it in the variable *jul*, computing the day of the week in the variable *day*. The return statement causes the function to finish, and *day* in *main()* takes the value of the variable *day* in the function *dow()*. The variable *day* in the function *dow()* is called that function's *return value.* You can think of the return value "replacing" the call to the function in the expression after the function has been called.

```
Perpetual Calendar
------------------

What month? 1
What year do you want the calendar for? 1984

 Su  M Tu  W Th  F Sa
--------------------
  1  2  3  4  5  6  7
  8  9 10 11 12 13 14
 15 16 17 18 19 20 21
 22 23 24 25 26 27 28
 29 30 31
```

A MORE COMPLETE CALENDAR

DESCRIPTION

The calendar program presented in the last section works fine, but it lacks a few nice features. First, it doesn't print the month and year on the calendar it generates. Second, it stops after one run through the program. This version expands on the program in the previous section to add the missing features.

HOW IT WORKS

First, a new function called *title()* has been added. This function prints the month's name and the year as a title on the calendar. A large *switch-case* statement inside the function prints the appropriate name of the month according to the value of the variable month. The spacing of each month is designed to look centered over the calendar output. In the next chapter you'll write a function to center text automatically, but for now you have to type in the number of blanks you want in each month's name.

Second, the statements that make up *main()* in the previous program have been wrapped in a *while* loop in this version of the program. This allows them to be repeated as often as you like. The statement

```
while (1 == 1) {
```

programs an endless loop; the only way out of this program is to enter a zero when prompted for the month. The statement

```
if (m == 0) break;
```

accomplishes this, breaking out of the *while* loop when zero is entered. Because of this change, the prompt message for the month has been changed, too.

LISTING

```
/* Listing 2-7. Perpetual Calendar Version 2
   Revised version puts title on calendar and repeats
*/


main()
{
        int day, i;
        float m, m1, d, y, jul;

        while (1 == 1) {
                printf("\n\nWhat month (type 0 to quit)?");
                m = gf();
                if (m == 0) break;
                printf("What year do you want the calendar for?");
                y = gf();
                title(m, y);
                printf("\n Su M Tu W Th F Sa\n");
                dashes(22);
                d = 1;
                m1 = m;
                jul = julmdy(m, d, y);
                day = dow(jul);
                for (i = 0; i < day; i++) printf("   ");
                while (m1 == m) {
                        printf(" %2.0f", d);
                        if (day == 6) printf("\n");
                        jul = jul + 1;
                        m1 = mjul(jul);
                        day = dow(jul);
                }
                printf("\n");
        }
}
```

```
title(m, y)                    /* put a nice title on the calendar */
float m, y;
{
        int month;

        month = m;
        printf("\n    ");
        switch (month) {
        case 1:  printf("  January ");
                 break;
        case 2:  printf(" February ");
                 break;
        case 3:  printf("    March ");
                 break;
        case 4:  printf("    April ");
                 break;
        case 5:  printf("      May ");
                 break;
        case 6:  printf("     June ");
                 break;
        case 7:  printf("     July ");
                 break;
        case 8:  printf("   August ");
                 break;
        case 9:  printf("September ");
                 break;
        case 10: printf("  October ");
                 break;
        case 11: printf(" November ");
                 break;
        case 12: printf(" December ");
                 break;
        }
}
```

SAMPLE RUN

```
What month (type 0 to quit)? 10
What year do you want the calendar for? 1984
```

```
        October 1984
   Su  M Tu  W Th  F Sa
   --------------------
    1  2  3  4  5  6  7
    8  9 10 11 12 13 14
   15 16 17 18 19 20 21
   22 23 24 25 26 27 28
   29 30 31

Enter the month (Type 0 to Quit)? 0
```

WHAT YOU LEARNED IN CHAPTER 2

You've covered a lot of ground in this chapter. Here are the new C statements you've seen, along with a brief description of what they do:

int	declares integer variables
else	specifies false statement for *if*
{ }	compound statement
while	execute statement while condition is true
switch	*switch-case* statement
break	immediately exit *for, while,* or *switch*
+ +	increment variable by 1

While this chapter has covered a lot of new concepts, they are almost all the special concepts you'll be needing before you start to program in C. Make sure you understand them by rereading the examples in this chapter before you go on.

In the next chapter, you learn how C can be used to process words in addition to time and money.

Working with Text
3

Until now, the programs you've seen have used numeric data exclusively. Occasionally you've enclosed text messages in quotation marks for printing (such as "Lease/Purchase Decision\n"), but for the most part your programs have dealt with numbers and calculations.

In most business applications you have to work with text as often as you do numbers. For example, you need to enter and store a customer's name, address, and credit references when you process a mortgage loan application. In this chapter, you learn how to use *character variables*, *character arrays*, and *strings* to handle text. You will write a function to print a string as a mailing label, and you will use two new utility functions, *fill()* and *center()*, to accent and center the calendar you developed in the last chapter.

CHARACTER VARIABLES

The basic unit of storage for text in C is the *character*. In most computers a single character takes up one byte of storage (see box). As with any other C variables, before you can use character variables, you must declare them.

V

Character Data

Character data occupies one byte per character. A character is usually represented using the American Standard Code for Information Interchange, or ASCII (pronounced ask-ee). The ASCII code assigns unique meanings to each of the 255 characters that can be represented in a single byte.

C compilers for the IBM System/370 series of computers use a different code to represent characters, the Extended Binary Coded Decimal Interchange Code, or EBCDIC (pronounced eb-see-dick). This code assigns completely different meanings to the 255 possible characters.

Because these character sets are different, you should avoid hex values for characters in your programs. Always use the symbols \t, \n, etc.

To declare a character variable, you put the word *char* in front of it. For example, to declare the variable *a* as a character, you use:

```
char a;
```

In this example, *a* holds a single character. You indicate a single character as data in C by enclosing it in single quotation marks. To assign the single character *D* to the character variable *a*, you use the statement

```
a = 'D';
```

A character can be a letter ('d' or 'D'), a digit ('4'), a punctuation symbol (';'), or any one of the 256 ASCII characters.

There are three things to remember. First, character data in C is case sensitive. In the previous assignment statement, an uppercase 'D' is not the same as a lowercase 'd'. As you write your programs, you will often need to check if a given character is uppercase or lowercase, alphabetic or numeric, or something else. You will acquire several handy functions for use in working with characters as you work through the examples in this chapter.

Second, there are some special characters used in C that cannot be represented with a single keystroke. You've already seen one such special character in the comments you've printed with the *printf()* function. This is the character *newline*, the \n you've often seen at the end of the messages. A newline combines a carriage return and a linefeed and is used to end a line of output and resume printing on the line below it. Even though a newline is really two characters (carriage return and linefeed), it is treated in C as one character with the ASCII value of 10 (corresponding to a single linefeed). C takes care of the translation for you if you use the symbol \n.

The backslash (\) is called the *escape character* in C. It is used to form several special characters including:

\t   tab character (ASCII value 9)

\b   backspace character (ASCII value 8)

\f   formfeed character (ASCII value 11)

\0   null character (ASCII value 0)

\\	single backslash
\'	single quotation mark
\"	double quotation mark

The null character (\0), which looks useless at first glance, is really a powerful programming tool; you learn more about its use in the next few sections.

CHARACTER ARRAYS

Although we need to store and retrieve single characters in our programs, it would be far too time-consuming if we had to declare a unique variable for each character in a customer's name or address. Fortunately, C lets us group a set of characters together under a single variable name. Such a variable is called an *array*.

An array reserves successive characters of memory under a single variable name. To declare a character variable to be an array, you list the number of characters you want the array to hold along with the array name. To declare *city* as a character array of no more than 10 characters, write:

```
char city[10];
```

This statement tells C to reserve 10 characters of memory under the name *city* in your program. As with any other C statement, the punctuation must appear in the statement *exactly* as shown. You must use the square brackets instead of the parentheses so that C can tell that *city* is an array and not a function.

Once you've defined an array, you can look at the individual characters stored in it by enclosing the position of the character you want in brackets, as in *city[1]* or *city[6]*. For example, if the array *city* held the characters "New York," then city[0] = N, city [1] = e, and so forth. (Note that the numbering of character positions in an array begins with 0.) As you might suspect, you can also enclose expressions in brackets, such as *city[i+1]*. An array name and an expression in brackets to indicate a character's position is called an *array element*. As a rule, you can use a character array element wherever you would use a single character.

STRINGS

So far, you've learned how to reserve space to hold several characters of data under a single variable name. It would be far too time-consuming if we had to assign each character separately to an array, as in the following listing:

```
char name[10];

name[0] = 'N';

name[1] = 'e';

name[2] = 'w';

name[3] = ' ';
```

and so forth.

Fortunately, you can fill an entire array with one instruction through the use of a *character string,* as in

```
strcpy(city, "New York");
```

A string in C is a set of characters, placed in a character array, that ends in a null character (the seemingly useless character \0 mentioned earlier). The null character is used to indicate the end of a string to the C compiler or interpreter. It allows us to write and use character functions in C without knowing how long a character string is beforehand. We simply instruct the program to process all characters from the start of the array up to the \0 character.

In C, double quotation marks are used to enclose a string. The characters in the string are automatically followed by the null character. You've already used quoted strings in your previous programs, in statements such as

```
printf("Lease/Purchase Decision\n");
```

These quoted strings had no variable name—they were simply passed to the function *printf(),* which displayed them. Such strings, not assigned to character arrays, are called *string constants.* There is a problem.

Franz & Good: Writing Business Programs in C Language (Chilton)

WORKING WITH TEXT

Because the string has no name, you have no way of accessing a specific character in the string.

The *strcpy()* function lets us assign a string constant to a character array. This function takes two arguments, the array variable name and the string constant. It copies all the characters in the string constant to the character array variable. To assign "New York" to *city*, for example, you'd write:

```
char city[10];

strcpy(city, "New York");
```

and now you can refer to *city[0]* and get N.

To get a string from the keyboard for use in the desktop calendar, you may recall having used the function *gets()*. The name of the variable you pass to *gets()* is the name of the array where the string will be placed after it has been read.

You must reserve (declare) as many spaces in memory as the longest possible string you will be reading. Declaring 10 characters won't help you if you've left your heart in "San Francisco." By the same token, we require a function that will tell us the number of characters in a character string, since this will usually be less than the number of characters that were allocated. This function is *strlen()*.

In the previous example, *city* was declared to be an array that could hold as many as 10 characters:

```
char city[10];
```

If you then assign *city* to "New York," you can print the length of the string as follows:

```
strcpy(city, "New York");

printf("%d", strlen(city));
```

and the result is 8.

The function *strlen()* begins with the first character in the array (city[0] in this example) and counts up, stopping when it encounters the character \0. The character \0 itself is not counted.

√

The *printf( )* Function

The function *printf()* is a versatile output formatting function. It has the following general form:

```
printf(format, item1, item2, . . . );
```

The items can be variables, integer constants, quoted strings, floating-point constants, characters, or even expressions.

The format is a quoted string containing ordinary characters, which are copied unchanged to the terminal, and format specifications. Format specifications begin with a % and end with a letter telling the type of field to format. The types used in this book are:

        f   for floating-point data

        d   for integer data

        s   for string data

        c   for character data

Between the % and the letter, you can enter (1) a number telling the width of the field or (2) in the case of floating-point data, the overall precision, a decimal point, and a number telling the number of digits to follow the decimal.

You will use the three functions *gets()*, *strcpy()*, and *strlen()* whenever you load and manipulate text.

MAILING LABELS

DESCRIPTION

This program takes a string entered from your terminal and formats it as a mailing label. The rule is simple: anywhere a backslash (\) is found in the string, a new line begins. As an example, if you enter an address block like this

```
Marty Franz\525 W. Walnut\Kalamazoo MI 49007
```

it will be printed like this

```
Marty Franz
525 W. Walnut
Kalamazoo MI 49007
```

HOW IT WORKS

The program consists of a *main()* function that reads and examines each string and a *label()* function that prepares and prints the mailing label. When you add the label function to the data-handling routines you will develop in Chapters 4 and 6, you'll have a general mailing-labels program you can use for your correspondence or a mass mailing to customers and prospective clients.

The main program reads a string of characters and passes it to *label()*. Inside *label()*, a *for* loop scans each string from the first character (s[0]) up to the last character, which is computed by taking *strlen(s)*. If a backslash (\) is encountered, a newline (\n) is printed instead. Otherwise, the character itself is printed with *printf()*. Extra *printf()* functions before and after the *for* loop ensure that lines are skipped before and after the label. When the user presses the RETURN key without entering any characters, the program terminates.

There are two unusual things to note in *label()*. The first is that you can print single characters with *printf()* by using the format "%c". The second is the declaration of *s* in the function header:

```
label(s)
char s[];
```

The empty brackets mean that the size of *s* will be determined by the function's caller. This makes sense since *label()* can be called from many different places in the program, with strings declared to many different sizes. Whenever you want to pass a string whose length you can't know in advance, you can declare it in the function header in this way.

LISTING

```
/* Listing 3-1. Mailing Label Program
   User enters a string containing \s, which is formatted
   as a mailing label
*/


main()
{
        char lbl[80];

        while (1 == 1) {
                printf("Label: ");
                gets(lbl, 80);
                if (strlen(lbl) == 0) break;
                label(lbl);
        }
}


label(s)        /* format string s as a mailing label */
char s[];
{
        int i;

        printf("\n"):
        for (i = 0; i < strlen(s); i++) {
        /* check for backslash "\" */
                if (s[i] == '\\')
                        printf("\n");
                else
                        printf("%c", s[i]);
        }
        printf("\n\n");    /* finish with newlines */
}
```

SAMPLE RUN

```
Label: Marty Franz\525 W. Walnut\Kalamazoo MI 49007

Marty Franz
525 W. Walnut
Kalamazoo MI 49007

Label:
```

NOTES

Now that we are working with text, we need to be able to read a line or more of characters at one time. The solution is a new input function, *gets()*. For example,

```
gets(lbl, 80);
```

gets a string of characters from the keyboard up to one line or 80 characters in length and saves them in lbl.

Because the *printf()* function treats the backslash as a control character, we must use \\ instead of just \ to scan the text for a backslash, as in the statement

```
if (s[i] == '\\')
```

FILLING AND CENTERING TEXT

You can modify the calendar program presented in the last chapter to center the name of the month and display a series of dashed lines. Two functions are required: *fill()* to create the dashed lines and *center()* to perform the centering. We will use both functions repeatedly whenever we wish to prepare reports for general distribution (see Chapter 7).

In what follows, you develop the two functions independently and then combine them with the program you developed earlier.

FILLING TEXT

When you're programming you often need to create strings of a fixed length containing all one character. An example is a long string of dashes for report headings. The next function, called *fill()*, makes a string filled with all one character. This function has three arguments: (1) the name of the string to fill, (2) the number of characters to fill, and (3) the character to fill with. To make an 80-character string of dashes, you'd write

```
char dash[80];
fill(dash, 80, '-');
```

HOW IT WORKS

Like *label()*, the *fill()* function scans the string from start (0) to end, as determined by *strlen(s)*, with a *for* loop. The single character *c* is inserted in each position of the string. Notice that the last position of the string is filled with \0, so that the string is terminated properly.

LISTING

```
/* Listing 3-2. Fill String with Character */

fill(s, m, c)          /* fill string s with character c */
char s[];
int m;
char c;
{
                          m
        int i;
        for (i=0; i<1; i++){
                s[i]=c;
        }
        s[m] = '\0';
}
```

There's no sample run here because you'll be testing this function later in this chapter as part of your improved calendar program.

CENTERING TEXT

The next function you're going to write centers one string inside another. You use this function whenever you put centered page titles on your

Franz & Good: Writing Business Programs in C Language (Chilton)

WORKING WITH TEXT

reports. The goal here is to develop a function called *center()* that takes as its arguments two strings: one to contain the heading string, which has already been made to length and filled properly with *fill()*, and one containing the title string to center in it. Using *fill()* and *center()* together, you can make centered headings as follows:

```
char heading[80];
fill(heading, 80, ' ');
center(heading, "Report Title");
printf(heading);
```

HOW IT WORKS

The *center()* function has two steps to it. The first step determines where the title string should be centered in the heading string; the second copies the title to the heading at that point. The spot where the title should be placed is computed by subtracting the length of the title from the length of the heading and then dividing by two. The variable *pos* keeps track of where in the heading the current character in the title selected by *i* should be placed. Notice how *pos* is incremented with ++ in the assignment statement that copies the character from the title into the heading.

LISTING

```
/* Listing 3-3. Center One String in Another */

center(h, t)                    /* center title t in heading h */
char h[], t[];
{
        int i, pos;

        pos = (strlen(h) - strlen(t))/2;
        for (i = 0; i < strlen(t); i++) {
                h[pos++] = t[i];
        }
}
```

Once again, there's no sample run. You'll be testing and using this function in the next section.

THE IMPROVED CALENDAR

DESCRIPTION

Now we are ready to modify the calendar program we developed in the last chapter by adding a series of dashed lines and centering the name of the month. The next listing and sample run show the results of our efforts.

HOW IT WORKS

In the listing below, some of the statements in the *main()* function for the calendar have been replaced with calls to *fill()*. In addition, the function *title()* has been rewritten to use the functions *strcpy()*, *fill()*, and *center()* to display the title for the calendar. In the *switch-case* statement, *strcpy()* is used to copy the name of the correct month into the character array *mname;* then this string is centered into *head* for the calendar heading.

LISTING

```
/* Listing 3-4. Perpetual Calendar Version 3
   Revised version puts centered title and dashes on calendar
*/


main()
{
        char dash[23];
        int day, i;
        float m, m1, d, y, jul;

        fill(dash, 22, '-');
        while (1 == 1) {
                printf("\n\nWhat month (type 0 to quit)");
                m = gf();
                if (m == 0) break;
                printf("What year do you want the calendar for");
```

```
                          y = gf();
                          if (y == 0) break;
                          printf("\n\n%s\n", dash);
                          title(m, y);
                          printf("%s", dash);
                          printf("\n Su M Tu W Th F Sa\n");
                          printf("%s\n", dash);
                          d = 1;
                          m1 = m;
                          jul = julmdy(m, d, y);
                          day = dow(jul);
                          for (i = 0; i < day; i++) printf("   ");
                          while (m1 == m) {
                                  printf(" %2.0f", d);
                                  if (day == 6) printf("\n");
                                  jul = jul + 1;
                                  m1 = mjul(jul);
                                  day = dow(jul);
                          }
                          printf("\n%s\n", dash);
                  }
        }


title(m, y)                    /* put a nice title on the calendar */
float m, y;
{
        char head[23], mname[23];
        int month;

                  month = m;
                  switch (month) {
                  case 1:  strcpy(mname,   "January");
                           break;
                  case 2:  strcpy(mname,   "February");
                           break;
                  case 3:  strcpy(mname,    "March");
                           break;
                  case 4:  strcpy(mname,    "April");
                           break;
                  case 5:  strcpy(mname,     "May");
                           break;
                  case 6:  strcpy(mname,    "June");
                           break;
```

```
          case 7:  strcpy(mname,        "July");
                   break;
          case 8:  strcpy(mname,      "August");
                   break;
          case 9:  strcpy(mname, "September");
                   break;
          case 10: strcpy(mname,    "October");
                   break;
          case 11: strcpy(mname,    "November");
                   break;
          case 12: strcpy(mname,    "December");
                   break;
          }
          fill(head, 22, ' ');
          center(head, mname);
          printf("%s\n", head);
          printf("            %4.0f\n", y);
}
```

SAMPLE RUN

```
What month (type 0 to quit)? 2
What year do you want the calendar for? 1984


----------------------
          February
            1984
----------------------
  Su  M Tu  W Th  F Sa
----------------------
             1  2  3  4
  5  6  7  8  9 10 11
 12 13 14 15 16 17 18
 19 20 21 22 23 24 25
 26 27 28 29
----------------------


What month (type 0 to quit)? 0
```

WHAT YOU LEARNED IN CHAPTER 3

In this chapter, you learned how to work with text in your C programs. You learned about the three ways text is stored in C: through character variables, arrays, and strings. In addition, you learned these C statements and functions:

char	declares character variables
[]	specifies array elements
strcpy()	copies one string to another
strlen()	returns length of a string

Finally, you wrote several functions to process text. The first of these printed a string as a mailing label, using the single backslash (\) as a flag to skip to a new line. You also wrote the functions *fill()* and *center()*, which you used to display and center the title for the calendar you developed in the last chapter.

In the next chapter, you begin to write programs that exceed a single page of C program listing. To simplify your work, you learn several valuable techniques for organizing and testing larger programs. The program you develop in the next chapter will be used in Chapters 5, 6, and 7 as well, so you'll want to pay close attention to its development.

An Electronic Checkbook 4

In the last three chapters, you developed a series of short programs that work with the three essentials of business: time, words, and money. While doing so, you learned the formats of almost all the statements you need to write programs in C. You learned to manipulate numbers and text and to structure your programs into a series of functions. And you learned the importance of proper syntax. In this chapter, you apply what you've learned to the development of a general-purpose checkbook program. By the time this chapter is over, you'll be able to enter, change, and delete deposits from your electronic checkbook and list the transactions on file. In later chapters, you will learn how to extend and modify your checkbook program so that you can find and sort checks, print a check register, and compute the float.

PROGRAMMING TECHNIQUES

The programs you've created so far have been relatively simple, taking no more than a page or two to list. The checkbook program you will develop in this chapter is much larger. To successfully write and test a program of this size you need additional techniques for designing, testing, and writing large programs.

ENGLISH-LANGUAGE DESCRIPTION

The first of these techniques is one you will use at the beginning of any new programming project. It consists of writing an English-language description of the program's function arranged like you would a *main()* program. The idea is to sit down and organize on paper the steps needed in the program. Don't worry about using correct C syntax now: all you want to do is describe what the program is supposed to do in general terms. For the checkbook program, for example, the initial English-language description might look like this:

```
set up everything needed
until done:
        ask what to do next
        if enter a check
                enter check information
        if delete a check
                enter check number
                find it
                delete it
        if change a check
                enter check number
                find it
                edit it
                enter new check information
                insert it in the checkbook
        if get checks
                load checks from file
        if save checks
                save checks to file
        otherwise
                print an error message
go ask again
```

Already you can see two benefits of this technique. First, your attention is drawn to statements that appear in the description more than once, like "enter check number" and "find it." Statements that are repeated frequently are good candidates for C functions. Second, you identify programming tasks you don't know how to do yet, such as "load checks from file" and "save checks to file." These tasks will require additional study.

Franz & Good: Writing Business Programs in C Language (Chilton)

AN ELECTRONIC CHECKBOOK

LEFT-CORNER CONSTRUCTION

Our second design technique employs what is called "left-corner" construction. This technique helps us organize the flow of our work. You begin by breaking off the "left corner" (some small part) of the problem and writing a small self-contained program to test it. Once that part is working, you attack the "left corner" of what remains. Eventually, there are no corners left, and the program is complete. You will use the left-corner approach throughout the construction of our checkbook program.

The tricky part of left-corner construction is determining a starting point. You want to use a section of the program small enough so that you can write it quickly and accurately, yet large enough so that you can test it without writing a lot of scaffolding. For the checkbook program, the minimum working program consists of three functions: (1) a *main()* function, since all C programs must have one of these; (2) an *add()* function that enters checks into the checkbook; and (3) a *list()* function that lists the checks. Without the *list()* function, writing the *add()* function is pointless, since you'd have no way to tell if it works. And the effort required to write a scaffold for listing checks may as well be put into writing the real listing function instead.

MAIN PROGRAM

DESCRIPTION

Despite the lengthy English-language description of *main()* on page 64, it has only two purposes. First, it initializes global variables such as *top* that mark the beginning of the checks in memory. Second, it acts as a traffic dispatcher; it requests a single-letter command that signifies which of the various program functions you want (such as add checks, list checks, etc.), and then it calls functions such as *add()*, *list()*, *load()*, or *save()* to do the dirty work. Since you've used a *main()* function to perform these tasks in earlier programs, you'll find this *main()* function easy to write.

HOW IT WORKS

The variable *_mend* is not declared below because it is already declared in the C libraries. The variable *_mend* contains the address of the character that marks the end of the array. You learn about variables that contain addresses in Chapter 6, page 98. All you need to know for now is that the statement

```
top = _mend;
```

sets the variable *top* to this address before any checks are added, thus marking the beginning of the checkbook.

The variable *top* is declared in the statement

```
unsigned top;
```

which appears before the opening brace that marks the *main()* function's beginning. This way all the functions in the checkbook program can access the information stored in it. Such a variable, recognized without further declaration everywhere in a program, is called a *global variable* in C. If a variable with the same name is declared inside a particular funciton, then only the inside-function variable gets updated with new information, not the global one. Because of the confusion this can cause, *avoid using the same names for global and local variables in your programs.* There are plenty of names to go around. The "localness" or "globalness" of a variable in C is sometimes called its *scope.*

The variable *top* is declared as an unsigned variable. In C, an unsigned variable is an integer that can take on only positive values. These have wider range than signed variables and can take any value from 0 to 65,535. A signed variable (an *int*) is restricted to values between −32,768 and 32,767. Unsigned variables are often used to store addresses.

The new function *toupper()* converts a single character to uppercase. We'll use this new function often to help make our programs user friendly. Remember that character data in C is case sensitive and that you have to convert data explicitly to the case you want for comparisons in *ifs, switches,* and *whiles.* We use the *toupper()* function so that you can type an *A* or an *a* and still get the result you desire.

The variable *top* is set to the end of memory initially, and then a *while (1 == 1)* loop is used in which you are asked which checkbook function you wish to perform. A *switch-case* statement is used to select the appropriate function. Exit from the program is done with the X command, which uses the standard function *exit()* to leave the program.

V

Variable Scope

Scope is the range of statements in your program over which you can use a variable's name. The rules for variable scope are:

1. Variables declared outside all functions are considered global and can be used anywhere in the program unless overridden by a local variable with the same name.

2. Variables declared in the body of a function (that is, between the braces) can be used in that function only.

3. Variables declared in the header of a function can be used in that function only.

Unsigned Numbers

Unsigned numbers in C usually occupy two bytes. This provides for a range of 0 to 65,535.

Unsigned constants are a string of digits without a sign. Since unsigned numbers often represent machine addresses that are in hexadecimal, you can specify hex numbers by putting *0x* in front of the number. Examples of unsigned constants are:

0,   1,   4023,   0xe000,   0xa4

```
/* Listing 4-1. Checkbook main() Function */

unsigned top;

main()
{
        char c[80];
        int num;
        unsigned p;

        top = _mend;    /* save start of memory */

        while (1 == 1) {
                printf("\nA)dd, L)ist, D)elete, C)hange, S)ave,
                   G)et, e(X)it: ");
                gets(c, 80);
                if (strlen(c) == 0) break;

                switch (toupper(c[0])) {
                case 'A':
                        add();
                        break;
                case 'L':
                        list();
                        break;
                case 'D':
                        num = ask();
                        p = find(num);
                        if (p != 0 ) delete(p);
                        break;
                case 'C':
                        num = ask();
                        p = find(num);
                        if (p != 0) {
                                printf("Old: %s\n", p);
                                delete(p);
                                printf("New: ");
                                gets(c, 80);
                                insert(c, p);
                        }
                        break;
```

```
            case 'S':
                    save();
                    break;
            case 'G':
                    load();
                    break;
            case 'X':
                    exit(0);
                    break;
            default:
                    break;
            }
        }
}
```

You can't run this program until you have the *add()* and *list()* functions.

ADDING CHECKS

DESCRIPTION

The first function you need to write adds new checks to the checkbook. This function implements the English description "enter check information." Since "enter check information" will require several C statements, a separate function, *add()*, is called for. For simplicity, no search is done in *add()* to see if the check is a duplicate. Instead, the new check is added to the end of the checkbook, with no further processing attempted.

HOW IT WORKS

The *add()* function first reads a character string (with a *gets()* function), checks to see if it is nonempty (with an *if* statement), and then inserts the string at the end of the checkbook register. (If the user presses RETURN without entering information, the string is empty, signaling the end of input to the program.)

The *insert()* function manipulates character data in a large character array in memory. This array is defined to be 8,192 characters, enough memory to store several dozen checks. The *insert()* function adds a string to this array. The variable *_mend* "points to" the last character in the array.

The *insert()* function is in most standard C libraries; if your C compiler lacks an *insert()* function, type in the listing provided in Appendix II.

LISTING

```
/* Listing 4-2. Checkbook add() Function */

add()
{
        char buf[80];

        printf("\nEnter your data:\n\n");
        while (1 == 1) {
                gets(buf, 80);
/* read in a character string */
                if (strlen(buf) == 0) break;
/* insert the string at the bottom of the register */
                insert(buf, _mend);
        }
}
```

NOTES

The listing contains a rather curious statement:

```
while (1 == 1) {
```

Because 1 is always equal to itself, this loop will go on forever! Actually, the loop terminates as soon as the user presses RETURN without entering any additional information. Instead of arranging for an exit from the loop by having the *while* condition turn false, we've used an *if* statement within the body of the loop to transfer control:

```
if (strlen(buf) == 0)) break;
```

This *while* statement is an example of what C linguists call an "idiom" of the language: a shorthand way of doing things that has become accepted through repeated use.

As you've noticed, you can't test the *add()* function yet. You need a function to list the checks again to see if they've been added correctly.

LISTING CHECKS

DESCRIPTION

This function will implement the line in our English-language description that reads: "list all the checks in the checkbook." Since it looks as if we'll need several statements to do this, a complete, separate function is called for. Simply put, the *list()* function goes through the checkbook and uses *printf()* to print each check.

HOW IT WORKS

The unsigned variable *p* in the function *list()* is set to the value *top*, the first character of the first check in the checkbook. As *p* is incremented throughout the program, a *while* loop is used to check *p* against the last character of the last check in the checkbook, contained in *_mend*. Since every string in C is terminated with a null character (\0), the loop checks for the next to last character, comparing *p* with (*_mend-1*) instead of *_mend*. Inside the *while* loop, the checks are printed by *printf()*.

Notice that the *strlen()* function is used to add the number of characters in the string "pointed at" by *p* to *p*. This lets us point *p* at the first character of the next string in the checkbook. We add 1 to the length of the string to account for the \0 at the end.

LISTING

```
/* Listing 4-3. Checkbook list() Function */

list()
{
        unsigned p;

        p = top;
        printf("\n");
        while (p < (_mend-1)) {
                printf("%s\n", p);
                p = p + strlen(p) + 1;
        }
}
```

SAMPLE RUN

Finally there is enough of a program to test. You can now add checks and then list them:

```
A)dd, L)ist, D)elete, C)hange, S)ave, G)et, e(X)it: a

Enter your data:

308 64.79 Dan Brown-cat bite victim
309 67.00 HILA
310 42.61 Kalamazoo City Treasurer-water bill

A)dd, L)ist, D)elete, C)hange, S)ave, G)et, e(X)it: 1

308 64.79 Dan Brown-cat bite victim
309 67.00 HILA
310 42.61 Kalamazoo City Treasurer-water bill

A)dd, L)ist, D)elete, C)hange, S)ave, G)et, e(X)it: c
```

NOTES

We have not said anything so far about the nature of the string that makes up the check. Is there a date, then an amount, and then a description? As far as this program is concerned, it does not make any difference how the data is entered within the string. Each string is saved in the checkbook and listed exactly as it is entered. As a result, our program is useful for storing a variety of records other than checks, from telephone numbers and addresses to lists of parts. In fact, you'll be using this program for more general record keeping beginning in the next chapter.

As you can see, the program has already grown beyond our ability to enter and test a single function. When this happens, it is essential that you write down specifications for each part of the program as you go so that you can be sure each piece that you add fits with the previous ones. Luckily, all the remaining parts of this program can be added and tested a function at a time. That's because the first "left corner" chosen allowed for easy expansion of the program.

DELETING CHECKS

DESCRIPTION

Now that you can add checks to the checkbook, you need some way to change checks or delete them altogether if you make a mistake. Without the ability to replace or delete erroneous data, a program isn't very useful. In the next two sections, you write the statements needed to delete and modify checks. You're adding the *delete()* function to the program first because it is the simpler of the two. How can you tell? By looking back at the English description you wrote at the start of the chapter:

```
if delete a check
    ask for check number
    find it
    delete it
else if change a check
    ask for check number
    find it
    delete it
    enter a new check
    insert it in the checkbook
else . . .
```

The lines "ask for check number" and "find it" are repeated in both sections of the description. After you write these functions to use in deleting a check, you can use them again to alter a check. This is because when a check is altered in this program it is deleted first, then replaced with a new copy. Note that the only functions not common to both changing and deleting checks are in the changing function, which is described in the next section (page 78).

In this section, we're going to deviate a bit from previous practice. You have been writing complete functions, such as *add()* and *list()*, to do each job and calling them in their entirety from *main()*. Because so few statements are needed to delete a check—only three statements in the English-language description—we write the code as several short C statements in *main()*. You can make them into a separate function, however, if you feel more comfortable with it that way.

There are two new functions. The first, *ask()*, asks for a check number from the user, reads it as a character string with *gets()*, converts it to an integer, and returns it to the caller, much like *gf()* does for floating-point numbers. Unlike *gf()*, *ask()* prompts the user with a message. In short, *ask()* takes care of the line in the description that reads "ask for check number."

The second function, *find()*, takes a check number as an argument and locates it in the checkbook, returning an unsigned integer that points to the check for a subsequent insertion or deletion. If the check isn't there, *find()* returns zero instead. The *find()* function implements the line in the English description that reads "find it." When you refer back to the listing, notice that the return value from *find()* is compared against zero back in *main()*. This ensures that if the check was not found, no attempt is made to delete it.

HOW IT WORKS

The function *find()* is important here, since it locates a check in memory starting from the beginning. A new function in *find()*, called *sscanf()*, is another workhorse function in C, so some discussion of it is called for.

In operation, *sscanf()* is the opposite of *printf()*. Where *printf()* prints a list of variables according to a specified output format, *sscanf()* scans a string and returns one or more variables back to you according to a specified input format. Using *sscanf()*, your programs can read text data and set program variables from it, which makes your programs far more flex-

The *sscanf( )* Function

The *sscanf()* function is a general-purpose input function. It extracts numeric variables from a string according to a format you provide. To call *sscanf()*, use:

sscanf(string, format, &var1, &var2, . . .);

where

string is the name of the string variable that has the data you want to convert,

format is a format similar to that used in *printf()*,

&var1 is the name of the variable in which to place the converted data.

You need to put & in front of your variable names because their addresses (not their values) are needed by *sscanf()* during conversion.

The input string is scanned from left to right. A blank terminates a field and moves scanning to the next variable in the list.

ible. The type conversions *(int, float)* are done by *sscanf()* for you auto-matically. A call to *sscanf()* looks like this:

```
sscanf(string, format, variables...);
```

The format part of *sscanf()* is similar to that used in *printf()*. In *find()*, you only need to get the first field of the string back as the check number (*i*), so the format is simple.

Most of the rest of the statements in *find()* are borrowed from *list()*. The *find()* function needs to go through the checks in the checkbook one by one, just as *list()* does. Instead of simply listing the checks, *find()* searches them. The *sscanf()* function converts the check number (which is assumed to be the first numeric field in the check) to *i*. The converted check number is compared against the check number you entered in *ask()*. If they are equal, the search stops and *p*, which points to the first character of the check, is returned to the calling function.

After the check is found, the *delete()* function is called to remove it, using the current value of *p*. Like *insert()*, *delete()* is contained in many standard C libraries. Please refer to Appendix II for a listing and if you need to add this function to your function library.

Notice that the revised program still assumes very little about the lay-out of the check. The only new assumption made by *find()* is that the first field in the check is a check number. The balance of the record can have any convenient format.

LISTING

```
/* Listing 4-4. Checkbook find() and ask() Functions */

ask()                    /* get a check number */
{
        int n;
        char num[80];

        printf("Check number: ");
        gets(num, 80);
        /* convert the string to an integer */
        n = atoi(num);
        return n;
}
```

```
find(n)            /* locate check number n */
int n;
{
        unsigned p;
        int i;

        p = top;
        while (p < (_mend-1)) {
                sscanf(p, "%d", &i);
                if (i == n) return p;
                p = p + strlen(p) + 1;
        }
        printf("That check is not on file\n");
        return 0;
}
```

NOTES

When the check number is encountered originally, it is part of a string of characters. The function *atoi()* (alphabetic to integer) converts the check number to an integer variable that can be added and subtracted. Thus *atoi()* would convert the string of characters 0, 2, 1 to 21.

SAMPLE RUN

```
A)dd, L)ist, D)elete, C)hange, S)ave, G)et, e(X)it: d

Check number: 2
A)dd, L)ist, D)elete, C)hange, S)ave, G)et, e(X)it: 1

308 64.79 Dan Brown-cat bite victim
310 42.61 Kalamazoo City Treasurer-water bill
```

CHANGING CHECKS

DESCRIPTION

The next function replaces a check with a new copy. You've actually already written this part—it's just lying in pieces over the rest of the program.

√

The *atoi( )* Function

You can convert a string containing digits and a sign into an integer with the *atoi()* (ASCII-to-integer) function. You pass *atoi()* the string, and it returns the converted integer from it:

int i;

i = atoi(" −2"); /* i = −2 */

Conversion begins with the first character in the string and ends with the first character that's not a digit or a sign. Leading blanks and tabs in the string are ignored, however.

The *atof( )* Function

You can convert a string containing digits, signs, and expo-
nents into a floating-point number with the *atof()* (ASCII-to-float-
ing point) function. You pass *atof()* the string and it returns the
converted floating-point number:

    float x;

    x = atof(" 10.0"); /* x = 10.0 */

Conversion begins with the first character in the string and ends
with the first character found that doesn't belong in a floating-
point number, be it blank, newline, or a nonnumeric character.
Leading blanks and tabs are ignored, however.

HOW IT WORKS

There's nothing new here. The *find()* and *delete()* parts were written in the last section, and the *add()* function was used to add new checks to the file. The big difference here is that instead of adding the check to the end of the file, you add the check at the point where the old one was deleted.

LISTING

```
/* Listing 4-5. New Code for main() to Change a Check
   Other functions already exist
*/
                case 'C':
                        num = ask();
                        p = find(num);
                        if (p != 0) {
                                printf("Old: %s\n", p);
                                delete(p);
                                printf("New: ");
                                gets(c, 80);
                                insert(c, p);
                        }
                        break;
        }
```

SAMPLE RUN

```
A)dd, L)ist, D)elete, C)hange, S)ave, G)et, e(X)it: c

Check number: 1
Old: 308 64.79 Dan Brown-cat bite victim
New: 308 64.79 Dan Brown

A)dd, L)ist, D)elete, C)hange, S)ave, G)et, e(X)it: 1

308 64.79 Dan Brown
310 42.61 Kalamazoo City Treasurer-water bill
```

NOTES

An important part of good software design is making sure that new features can be added easily to the program. Notice that after a "critical mass" of functions (adding checks, *main()*, listing checks) was written, each new part became easier to write. This last part was the easiest of all, since all the functions used were written earlier. You should aim for a similar flexibility in your own programs.

READING AND WRITING FILES

DESCRIPTION

The final two functions presented in this chapter load and save the checkbook through the use of files. To write these functions, you first need to know more about how C reads and writes to files.

In C, file input and output are done with four basic functions. The first, *fopen()*, sets up a file for input or output. Before you can read or write to a file, it must be "opened" so that your computer's operating system can identify the file's name and allocate memory for reading or writing data. The function *fopen()* has two arguments: the name of the file and the type of access you want, either "r" for read or "w" for write.

When you successfully open the file, *fopen()* returns a number called a *file descriptor*. This can be either a small integer or an address—there is no fixed convention, and different software/hardware combinations implement it in different ways. In this book, file descriptors will be declared as unsigned. The file descriptor is a shorthand way to refer to the file once it has been opened, in preference to using the complete name. With the file descriptor, your program can use the functions *fgets()* and *fprintf()* to read and write files.

Both *fgets()* and *fprintf()* work like their "normal" counterparts, *gets()* and *printf()*, except that they require the file descriptor for the file you want to read or write data to. For example, to read a string called *buf* from the terminal, you use the statement

```
gets(buf, 80);
```

To read *buf* from a file called "MYFILE", you would use instead

```
fd = fopen("MYFILE", "r");

fgets(buf, 80, fd);
```

Your program can tell if the file has reached its end by checking the value returned by *fgets()*. If valid data was read, *fgets()* returns the address of that data. If the file is at its end, or if an I/O error occurred, *fgets()* returns 0 instead.

Writing to the file is similar to using *printf()*. To write the string "Hi there" out to your terminal, you use:

```
printf("Hi there\n");
```

To do the same thing to the file "MYFILE", you use the statements

```
fd = fopen("MYFILE", "w");

fprintf(fd, "Hi there\n");
```

A word of caution: When you open a file for writing, C assumes that it is empty to begin with. If a file with the same name already exists, *fopen()* will erase it and create a new one. Check your file names before you run any of your programs.

The final file I/O function we need is *fclose()*. After a file has been completely read or written, your program must close it. This tells the operating system you are through with the file, so that it can free the memory allocated to it and "flush" any data that's not yet written to disk. To close a file, call *fclose()* with its file descriptor:

```
fclose(fd);
```

SUMMING UP

To use files in C, follow this five-step procedure:

1. Declare the variable for the file descriptor as an unsigned variable, and all the strings needed as *char* variables. You need a string for the file's name, and one for the data.

2. Open the file with *fopen()*. Save the file descriptor in the variable you declared.

3. Read the data with *fgets()*. When the end of file is reached, *fgets()* returns 0.

or

4. Write the file with *fprintf()*.

5. When your program is finished processing the file, close the file with *fclose()*.

HOW IT WORKS

The functions *load()* and *save()* are simple variations of the functions *add()* and *list()*. In each case, the user is asked to supply the name of the file. No error checking is done after *fopen()*, so it's up to the user to be sure the file name is a correct one. (This is not a good idea normally; we've done it here only to keep the listing simple.) The file descriptor is saved in *fd* and then used to read or write the file. The extra *printf()* functions display dots on the screen while loading or saving is going on. The process of loading or saving records can take several seconds; these dots give the user some reassurance that the program is not hung up in the interim but is executing according to plan.

The only unusual statement in these functions is in *load()*. Inside the *while* loop that reads data from the file you can see the statement

```
s[strlen(s)-1] = '\0';
```

This statement removes the \n appended to the end of each line of data when the file was saved. The expression [strlen(s)-1] points to the next-to-last character in the string s. By assigning this character to \0 (null), the statement shortens the string by one character, removing the \n.

LISTING

```
/* Listing 4-6. Checkbook load() and save() Functions */

load()                  /* load data into the array */
{
        char filename[80], s[80];
        unsigned p, fd;
```

```
                    _mend = top;              /* reset data stored */
                    printf("File name: ");
                    gets(filename, 80);
                    fd = fopen(filename, "r");
                    printf("Loading");
                    while (fgets(s, 80, fd) != 0) {
                            s[strlen(s)-1] = '\0';
                            insert(s, _mend);
                            printf(".");
                    }
                    fclose(fd);
                    printf("\n");
        }


        save()            /* save the file to disk */
        {

                    char filename[80];
                    unsigned p, fd;

                    printf("File name: ");
                    gets(filename, 80);
                    if (strlen(filename) == 0) return;
                    fd = fopen(filename, "w");
                    p = top;
                    printf("Saving");
                    while (p < (_mend-1)) {
                            fprintf(fd, "%s\n", p);
                            printf(".");
                            p = p + strlen(p) + 1;
                    }
                    printf("\n");
                    fclose(fd);
        }
```

SAMPLE RUN

```
A)dd, L)ist, D)elete, C)hange, S)ave, G)et, e(X)it: s
File name: stuff
Saving..
A)dd, L)ist, D)elete, C)hange, S)ave, G)et, e(X)it: g
File name: stuff
Loading..
```

Franz & Good: Writing Business Programs in C Language (Chilton)

AN ELECTRONIC CHECKBOOK

WHAT YOU LEARNED IN CHAPTER 4

You've covered a lot of ground in this chapter, but it's been worth it: your checkbook program is the basis for all the programs presented in future chapters. The functions presented in the rest of this book will all be add-ons to this basic program.

More important, you learned how to simplify the development of large programs by first writing an English specification and then breaking the job into small, easily tested pieces. With these techniques you can now approach almost any programming task.

You also learned how to use files in your C programs. Files are an essential part of all programs, and C provides a convenient way to use them through the functions *fgets()* and *fprintf()*.

The library functions you learned in this chapter are:

insert()	add strings to memory
delete()	delete strings from memory
strlen()	return length of string
toupper()	convert character to uppercase
sscanf()	format input
fopen()	open a file for processing
fclose()	close a file
fgets()	read strings from a file
fprintf()	write data to a file

In the next chapter, you write a general statistics program to make this checkbook program still more useful.

Business Statistics
5

In this chapter, you write a program that processes files created by your electronic checkbook and computes basic statistics, including the number of items in the checkbook, their total, their mean, and their standard deviation. The functions you develop can be applied to any set of numeric data for which statistics are required.

There are no new C language concepts presented in this chapter, but you learn more about the use of files in C, something that was only touched on in Chapter 4.

A PLAN FOR A STATISTICS PROGRAM

This program is much simpler than the checkbook program developed in the previous two chapters. The checkbook program had to load records into memory, edit them, and save them in a file. Our statistics program takes advantage of this previous effort and simply reads the file created by the checkbook program. An English-language description of this program might be:

> get a file name
> open the file
> while not at end of file

```
        read a record
        tally the record for statistics
repeat
compute final statistics
print final statistics
```

Your trained eye will notice that this description is somewhat vague about what "tally the record for statistics" means. In truth, we need to know more about the format of the record (something we skipped over in past chapters) before we can think about how to compute the statistics.

You may recall we assumed that the first field of each record would be for identification only: a check number, part number, or whatever. Statistics on these numbers, which are integer and will usually occur in sequence, won't be very useful. Likewise, the second and third fields may well be word descriptions, which we can't add or subtract. For simplicity, let's assume that the second field in each record is the first true "numeric data" field. (If it isn't, we can use the *sscanf()* function, described in Chapter 4, to get to the field we need.)

Now that we know *where* in the record the data will be, we can decide *what* statistics to keep. A few of the most useful are:

- The number of records processed

- The largest data item

- The smallest data item

- The sum of all the data items

- The average of all the data items

- The standard deviation

We've included these in the program listing below. Feel free to add other statistics you feel would be of value to you or your programming clients.

Let's take another look at the English-language description above. Note that the program reads one file, processes it, and exits. Often you will want to run the program a second or third time to process additional files. Rather than start the program from scratch each time, you'd like to be able to process one file and then loop back to ask for another one. To accomplish this, we wrap the statements in *main()* in a loop that will continue cycling until you want to stop processing files. We are also going to extract the statistics processing statements and put them in a separate function of their own. This will make it easier to add statistics to other programs we write.

Our new *main()* function looks like this:

```
while user wants to continue
    get a file
    process it
    close the file
    ask if user wants to go again
repeat
```

Our new "process it" function contains the statistics calculation statements taken out of the old *main()* and looks like this:

```
set up everything
while not at end of file
    read a record
    tally the record for statistics
repeat
compute final statistics
print final statistics
```

In this description, we are relying on *main()* to open and close the file and to pass the appropriate file descriptor to the statistics function file. In the last chapter, we relied on the user to enter the name correctly. This is a risky procedure, and we use this opportunity to add error-checking capability to *main()*. The new function will get the file's name from the user, open it, and then either return the file descriptor from *fopen()* or, if there was an error, ask the user for a file name a second time.

In English, this error check is set up like this:

```
file = bad
while file = bad
    get a file name
    if user just pressed return break
    open the file
    if file was opened ok file = good
```

```
repeat
if file = bad return 0
else return file descriptor
```

The statements "file = bad" and file = good" refer to settings of a variable that is used to control the *while* loop. Such a control variable, which holds no "real" quantities such as a name or an amount, is often called a "switch" because it functions just like a railroad switch does: in this case, the loop keeps looping until a good file name is received or the user presses RETURN without entering additional data. When either event occurs, the switch is thrown and the loop exits.

To summarize, here is a list of the functions we need to create for the statistics program:

main()   of course!

stats(fd)   processes statistics of file

getfile()   gets and opens a file and returns a valid file descriptor

again()   asks if you want to run the program again

Now, finally, you can start writing the program. Instead of using a left-corner approach, you're going to write the entire program from the *main()* function on down and test it as a unit. You write the *main()* function in the next section and the *getfile()*, *stats()*, and *again()* functions in the sections that follow. In this instance you can get away with this short-cut because the statistics program isn't as large or complicated as the checkbook program. Besides, you've seen and used all the C techniques in this program before, and, we hope, you've gained a lot of confidence in your own programming style.

THE *main* ( ) FUNCTION

DESCRIPTION

Our *main()* function is short and sweet and consists primarily of function calls. This isn't an accident but a result of our taking the time to prepare and organize an English-language description of the program before we began to write statements in C.

HOW IT WORKS

There's nothing new here. Notice that the file descriptor *fd* is declared as an unsigned variable, just as it was in Chapter 4. Of course, you can't run this program yet, since none of the subfunctions are written.

LISTING

```
/* Listing 5-1. Statistics main() Function */

main()
{

        int quit;
        unsigned fd;

        quit = 0;
        while (quit == 0) {
            fd = getfile();
            if (fd!=0)
                stats(fd);
                fclose(fd);
            quit = again();
            }
}
```

GETTING A FILE NAME

DESCRIPTION

The *getfile()* function gets a file name from the user, opens it, and returns the file descriptor back to the calling function if the *fopen()* was successful. If not, it displays an error message and asks for another file name. At any time the user can exit from the function by pressing ENTER and not typing anything else.

   The file is opened only for reading, not writing. If you want to open a file for writing, the procedure is more complicated, because you would need to check first to be sure that a file with the same name doesn't already exist. As mentioned in Chapter 4, if a file that is opened for writing has data in it already, the data will be written over and destroyed. To forestall the accidental destruction of essential data, have the program open the file for reading before it tries to open it for writing. If the read open was successful, you know the file is already there, and you can include a warning message to be displayed on the screen ("This file already exists. Write over it (Y/N)?").

HOW IT WORKS

When *fopen()* can't open a file, it returns a zero instead of returning a file descriptor. The *getfile()* function checks for this zero and takes appropriate action with an *if* statement. The variable *gotit* is a switch that controls the *while* loop. The function sets *gotit* to zero initially and then to 1 when a file has been successfully opened. Notice that we did not use the file descriptor in place of *gotit*, even though it too is zero until the file is opened and nonzero thereafter. Bitter experience has taught us *never to use a variable for more than one purpose in one program.* The file descriptor is an address. It should not be used as a switch.

LISTING

```
/* Listing 5-1. Statistics getfile() Function */

getfile()
{
        int gotit;
        unsigned fd;
        char filename[80];

        gotit = 0;
        fd = 0;
        while (gotit == 0) {
                printf("\nFile name: ");
                gets(filename, 80);
                if (strlen(filename) == 0) gotit = 1;
                else {
                        fd = fopen(filename, "r");
                        if (fd == 0)
                                printf("Can't open file: %s\n",
                                        filename);
                        else
                                gotit = 1;
                }
        }

}
```

You still can't test this program, since there are two more functions to write. So no sample run is shown yet.

PROCESSING STATISTICS

DESCRIPTION

The function *stats()* is the real meat of this program. It reads the file and computes the statistics. The formulas it uses for the statistics are:

For each record:
$$n = n + 1$$
$$total = total + data$$
$$sumsq = sumsq + pow(data, 2)$$

At the end of the file:
$$average = total/n$$
$$stddev = sqrt((sumsq - (pow(total, 2)/n))/(n - 1))$$

Where the variables are:

n	the number of data items
total	the sum of all data items
sumsq	the sum of their squares
average	their average
stddev	their standard deviation

The largest data item and the smallest data item are also computed. There's no formula for these; the function stores a value for each and updates it with the value in the new record if it's larger (smaller) than the existing value.

HOW IT WORKS

In structure, *stats()* looks like the *load()* function back in Chapter 4, since it reads the file until the end and processes each record. Notice that the variable *small* is assigned initially to 99999999. This guarantees that anything that is read into the program is likely to be smaller. Similarly, *large* is set equal to −9999999. Remember, *always pay careful attention to how your program's data is initialized.*

LISTING

```
/* Listing 5-3. Statistics stats() Function */

stats(fd)
unsigned fd;
{
        int n, i;
        char rec[80];
        float data, total, average, sumsq, small, large, stddev;

        n = 0;
        total = 0;
        average = 0;
        sumsq = 0;
        large = -9999999;
        small = 9999999;
        printf("\nReading");
        while (fgets(rec, 80, fd) 0) {
                sscanf(rec, "%d %f", &i, &data);
                n = n + 1;
                total = total + data;
                sumsq = sumsq + pow(data, 2.0);
                if (data < small) small = data;
                if (data > large) large = data;
                printf(".");
        }
        printf("\n");
        average = total/n;
        stddev = sqrt((sumsq - (pow(total, 2.0))/n)/(n-1));
        printf("There were %d records read\n\n", n);
        printf("The largest is........... %10.2f\n", large);
        printf("The smallest is.......... %10.2f\n", small);
        printf("The total is............. %10.2f\n", total);
        printf("The standard deviation is %10.2f\n", stddev);
}
```

SAMPLE RUN

You're almost there. If you wanted to, you could run the main program
now, simply by placing the call to *again()* in *main()* between opening and
closing /* /*. This would convert the call to a comment, which is ignored

when the program is executed. But be patient; *again()* is the shortest function in the program.

ASKING FOR ANOTHER

DESCRIPTION

Now you can tie up the remaining loose end and write *again()*. As you can see, it's not a very large function.

HOW IT WORKS

To simplify the program's use, you convert the first character to upper-case by *toupper()* before comparison against *Y*. As a result, it doesn't matter whether the caps lock is on or off: *y* or *Y* works equally well. This may seem a minor touch, but it is easily done and contributes greatly to the usability of the program. You could have used *strcmp()* here, checking for the whole string "yes" instead of just "y," but why type more? Also, you'd have to convert every character in the input string to uppercase, which would require writing yet another function.

LISTING

```
/* Listing 5-4. Statistics again() Function */

again()
{
        char yn[80];

        printf("\nDo you want to run again? (Y/N): ");
        gets(yn, 80);
        if (toupper(yn[0]) == 'Y') return 0;
        else return 1;
}
```

SAMPLE RUN: TESTING EVERYTHING

Now that the whole program has been entered, you can test it. First, you need to create some test data for it:

```
A)dd, L)ist, D)elete, C)hange, S)ave, G)et, e(X)it: A

Enter your data:

1   1   one
2   2   two
3   3   three
4   4   four
5   5   five
6   6   six
7   7   seven
8   8   eight
9   9   nine

A)dd, L)ist, D)elete, C)hange, S)ave, G)et, e(X)it: S
File name: statest
Saving.........
```

Notice that while the test data isn't very interesting, it does have the advantage of a known maximum, minimum, average, and standard deviation.

```
A)dd, L)ist, D)elete, C)hange, S)ave, G)et, e(X)it: G
File name: statest
Reading.........
There were 9 records read
The largest is...........      9.00
The smallest is..........      1.00
The total is.............     45.00
The average is...........      5.00
The standard deviation is      2.74

Do you want to run again? (Y/N): n
```

WHAT YOU LEARNED IN CHAPTER 5

It might seem unreasonable to you that the program presented in this chapter worked the first time. It's not. Barring typing errors (the nemesis of all programmers), there's no reason that a properly designed program can't work the first time it's tested. To get this to happen here, you've had to follow a highly specific procedure:

1. You wrote an English description of what the program was to do.
2. You analyzed that description to spot bugs and likely candidates for functions.
3. You wrote each function independently of the others.
4. You carefully tested pieces of the program as you saw the need for it, using known data.

Incidentally, now that you have a function for safely opening a file for reading, you might want to go back to the checkbook program presented in the last two chapters and modify it to use *getfile()* when a new file is loaded by *load()*. More generally, as you gain confidence and a deeper understanding of C, you may want to go back and modify all the programs we've created so far. Since you can do so much with these programs, any time you spend making them more convenient or reliable is worthwhile.

In the next chapter, you will write some additional functions for the checkbook program. These functions allow you to sort and select checks and perform more general record-keeping functions. In addition, you will use pointer variables, a powerful way to process strings.

============================

Record Keeping
6

In Chapter 4, you wrote a program to store, delete, and list the checks in your checkbook. Actually, the program you created is so general that it can be used for any record-keeping function, including maintaining lists of clients and prospects, tracking samples in a laboratory, and inventory control. In this chapter you add some additional functions that make your "little database" program more flexible and more useful for more kinds of applications. As you noticed in the last chapter, making your programs and functions more flexible has a lot of advantages in C, since it means you can use them over and over again.

First, you're going to add a selection function to your checkbook. You can use such a function to locate all deposits or a check you wrote for $200,000! (Two hundred thousand dollars! Let's hope it was an error at the bank.) You could also use such a function to select lists of prime prospects or to check on orders in a record of sales.

Next, you add a function that sorts the records in the checkbook so that they can be arranged and printed by check number or by data. (If you use your "little database" to maintain a list of prospects, the sort function will allow you to print out your mailing codes in zip code order.)

Last, you modify the checkbook program so that it can be used for a second application, a "Rolodex" file of employee names, phone numbers, and departments. The ability to adapt this program for a second, unanticipated use reflects the care we put into its design.

You have most of the C concepts under your belt by now. In this chapter, you fine tune what you've learned and discover how to increase the execution speed of your programs through the use of pointers.

POINTERS IN C

In this chapter we'll be working with character strings whose length cannot be forecast in advance, a feat we can accomplish only with the aid of *pointers.* In C terminology, any variable that contains an *address* in memory where data is stored is called a *pointer variable* or *pointer.* Pointers are used to access strings, important areas of memory in your computer such as your video screen, and arrays of integers and floating-point numbers.

Like other types of data in C, pointer variables have to be declared before you can use them. You declare a pointer by telling C the type of data it points at, and by using the character * in front of the pointer variable's name. For example, to declare the variable *p* as a pointer to character data, write

```
char *p;
```

in the start of your function. This tells C to reserve enough space for *p* to contain an addresss (usually two to four bytes of data) and to treat any references to *p* in the function as a reference to a single character.

Why go through this trouble? Why not just declare ''char p;'' instead? The advantage of a pointer is that it lets you point at successive characters in memory simply by incrementing the pointer's value. To access the next character in memory after *p*, for example, add 1 to *p*:

```
p = p + 1;
```

or

```
p++;
```

Now *p* contains the address of the character *after* the one you started with.

One alternative to pointers is to use subscripts as one does in FOR-TRAN or PL/1. In fact, you can do anything with pointers you can do with subscripted arrays. The advantage of the pointer is that you have to allocate memory space only for one value, the pointer, not for an entire array.

Computations that use pointer variables are called *pointer expressions* in C. You can always put a * in front of a pointer expression to access the data the result points at. For example, if you have a pointer called *next:*

```
char *next;
```

you can add three to next and access the character pointed to with a single statement

```
*(next+3)
```

There's a catch. In C, only one of the variables can be a pointer. That means you can't subtract two addresses, for instance, to find the number of characters between them. If you need to do calculations with addresses, as we do in the program below, you will have to copy one of the pointers to an unsigned variable. For example, in the last chapter, the variable __mend was really a pointer to the last character in the checkbook.

The address operator in C returns the address of a variable for use in assigning a pointer. The address operator is the character &, and it is placed in front of a variable. Here's an example:

```
char c, *p;      /* a character, and a pointer */

c = 'C';

p = &c;
```

After these statements are executed, *p* contains the address of *c* and *p* is the character *C*.

With these new concepts in mind, you can begin to select checks from the checkbook.

V

Pointers and Functions

A common use of pointers in C is to pass addresses of arguments to functions. This way, the function can assign values to the actual variables, effectively returning more than one value. You use this method of argument passing whenever you use *sscanf()* so that the function can fill in more than one variable from the input string.

That Funny &

The & symbol is called the *address operator* in C. It returns the address of the variable it is placed in front of. When you use an &, don't place a blank between it and the variable name.

To see how & works, study the following example. These two sets of C statements do the same thing:

```
float a, b, x;
x = func(a, b);

float func(a, b);
float a, b;
{
```

and

```
float a, b, x;
x = float(&a, &b);

float func(a, b);
float *a, *b;
{
```

Once the addresses of the variables are passed to the function, use pointers to get at the data.

SELECTING RECORDS

DESCRIPTION

The *select()* function presented here deletes all records in the checkbook that don't contain a specific key field. The task is complicated, and again we begin by writing an English-language description of our program:

> get key to search for
> start at first check
> while we still have checks
>   look for the key in the check
>   if not found delete the check
>   get next check
> repeat

This description glosses over the chief difficulty—finding the key in the check. We've never tried programming anything like this before. In fact, the comparison operators you learned previously, == and !=, won't on more than one character or number at a time! We can't use

```
char array1[5], array2[5];
```

and

```
if (array1 == array2) ...
```

to check *array1* and *array2* for equality.

Warning: If you write these statements anyway, C won't give you an error message. The *addresses* of *array1* and *array2*, not the values, will be compared. Address comparison is not at all what was intended. This is a common mistake, so be on the alert for it when writing programs that work with strings.

Luckily, you have a C function to help. The function *strcmp()* (string compare) compares two strings, returning 0 if the strings were equal, −1 if the first string is less than the second, and 1 if the first string is greater than the second.

With *strcmp()*, you can compare *array1* and *array2* like this:

```
if (strcmp(array1, array2) == 0) ...
```

The comparison goes character by character until one of the strings has a null in it. *Warning:* The strings have to be of equal length, contain characters in the same case (upper or lower), and have the same number of blanks on the end, too.

Now do you think the program will work? A simple version of the *select()* function is shown below:

```
select()
{
      char *p, key[80];

      gets(key, 80);
      p = top;
      while (p < (_mend-1)) {
            if (strcmp(p, key) == 0) delete (p);
            else p = p + strlen(p) + 1;
      }
}
```

This simple function works; the problem is that only records that match the key exactly get selected. But to be useful, the *select()* function should also select records in which any part of the record matches the key. Then you can select all the checks paid to a certain company regardless of their amount, and so on.

We must modify the function so that the key is compared against all the possible "pieces" of the record that can match it. How many pieces are there in a given record? If your record is "cat" and your key is "c," you have to match the key against c, a, and t in turn, since any single letter can match the key. If the key is "ca," you have to match it against ca and at, since both pairs of letters could match it. In all, the number of pieces you have to compare against the key is:

no. of characters in record − no. of characters in key + 1

or, saying it in C,

```
strlen(p) - strlen(key) + 1;
```

With this added wrinkle, the description for the new *select()* is:

get key to search for
start at first check
while you still have checks
    start at first piece of record
    while you still have pieces
        compare piece to key
        if found break
        else get next piece
    repeat
    if key was not found delete record
    get next check
repeat

And this is the version of *select()* presented here.

HOW IT WORKS

There are two new C ideas in this program. The first is the decrement operator (— —) seen in both *select()* and *strncpy()*. Do you remember that ++ increments a variable by one? Decrement subtracts one from the variable. It's a shorthand way of writing

```
i--;
```

instead of

```
i = i - 1;
```

The second new idea is having one *while* statement inside another. A simple or a compound statement can follow the *while* clause. In fact, you can have any number of *while* statements nested inside one another. Just watch your braces to see that they match.

There's a function in most C libraries called *strcpy()*, which copies one string to another. The function in this listing, *strncpy()* is more flexible and will copy any specified number of characters. The *while* loop in *strncpy()* checks for that number of characters (contained in the argument n and decremented), and just to be on the safe side, it checks that the string you're copying from has fewer than n characters in it.

Don't forget to add the new *select()* function to the *main()* function in your checkbook program so that it appears as a program option.

LISTING

```
/* Listing 6-1. Selection Functions for Checkbook Program
   select() removes records
   strncpy() copies parts of strings
*/


select()
{
        int dc, n;
        char *p, *s, key[80], work[80];

        printf("Key to select: ");
        if (gets(key, 80) == 0) return;
        p = top;
        dc = 0;
        printf("\n");
        while (p < (_mend-1)) {
                s = p;
                n = strlen(p) - strlen(key) + 1;
                while (n > 0) {
                        strncpy(work, s, strlen(key));
                        if (strcmp(work, key) == 0) break;
                        s++;
                        n--;
                }
                if (n == 0) {
                        delete(p);
                        dc++;
                }
                else {
                        printf("%s\n",p);
                        p = p + strlen(p) + 1;
                }
        }
        printf("%d records deleted\n", dc);
}
```

```
strncpy(t, s, n)          /* copy n chars from s to t */
char *t, *s;
int n;
{
        while (n > 0 && *s != '\0') {
                *t = *s;
                t++;
                s++;
                n--;
        }
}
```

SAMPLE RUN

A)dd, L)ist, D)elete, C)hange, s(E)lect, S)ave, G)et: a

Enter your data:

1 this is the contents of a record
2 this is the contents of another one
3 not here though

A)dd, L)ist, D)elete, C)hange, s(E)lect, S)ave, G)et: e

Key to select: this

1 this is the contents of a record
2 this is the contents of another one
2 records deleted

A)dd, L)ist, D)elete, C)hange, s(E)lect, S)ave, G)et:

NOTES

When you run the test of this function, you may notice that it runs verry sloowly. You can increase the speed of execution by modifying the program so as to "anchor" the key search to a specific character position in the record. Search only the characters after the tenth in the record, for example. This reduces the number of pieces to search and therefore speeds things up.

Interestingly, it doesn't seem to matter how long the key is: if the key is short, more pieces must be examined; if the key is long, more characters need to get copied.

SORTING RECORDS

DESCRIPTION

The functions presented in this section sort the records in the checkbook into ascending order. You supply a starting column to sort from, and the function does the rest.

To sort the checkbook, we need to copy every string into an array where it can be compared and moved to a new position if need be. After it is sorted, the checkbook needs to be rearranged in its new order. The complete sorting process can be thought of as three separate steps:

- Copy the records into an array

- Sort the array

- Rearrange the sorted records in the checkbook

In the program listing that follows, each step in the sorting process is given its own function. The function *readin()* scans the checkbook and copies each string to an array. The function *sort()* sorts this array, and the function *writeout()* arranges the checks back in the checkbook after they've been correctly sorted.

HOW IT WORKS

Before you can use these functions, you need to add two more global variables to your checkbook program ahead of *main()*:

```
char *recs[100];

int nrecs;
```

These new declarations allocate space for an array of 100 pointers (not an array of 100 characters) and for an integer called *nrecs*, which will contain the number of actual records in the checkbook. We put the declarations *outside* the main function because they are used by all three sorting functions. It's easier to declare both of them as global variables than to pass them back and forth among the functions.

The array *recs*, which consists of pointers to strings, is another illustration of the convenience and efficiency of pointer variables. We are using this array here to hold the address of every string in the checkbook. With the aid of this array, you can scan the checkbook quickly during the sort and perform such comparisons as

```
if (strcmp(recs[i], recs[j]) = = 1) ...
```

that compare two records in the checkbook against each other. *Remember:* You're only saving the addresses of the strings in *recs*, not the strings themselves.

The first function, *readin()*, goes through the checkbook starting at the beginning and saves a pointer for each record in *recs*. This loop should be familiar to you by now, since variations of it are used in *list()*, *find()*, *save()*, and *select()*—anywhere that the checkbook needs to be scanned record-by-record and processed. This loop increments *nrecs* as it goes so that the other two functions, *sort()* and *writeout()*, know how many records there are.

A new feature of C in this function can be seen in the statement:

```
recs[nrecs++] = p;
```

This single statement, with *nrecs* being incremented by the + + operator, does the same thing as the two statements:

```
recs[nrecs] = p;
```

```
nrecs = nrecs + 1;
```

Both these forms do the same thing; the first is easier to type while the second is easier to read. As you write more C programs, idioms like recs[nrecs++] become easier to comprehend. Still, use them only if you feel comfortable with them. The most important thing is that you understand what your programs are doing and that you can refer to the listings for guidance months or even years after they were first developed.

The function *sort()* takes the complete array *recs* and sorts it into ascending order by comparing strings with *strcmp()*. Before it begins the sort, it asks for a starting position within each record at which to begin the comparison. By altering the starting position, the user can sort a check's amount or the date as well as the check number. Such flexibility is invaluable for effective data management, as you'll see when we build a directory, similar to a Rolodex file, in the next section.

The sorting method used by the program is the so-called bubble sort. Two *for* loops scan the array. The outer *for* loop steps the variable *i* through every element in the array but the last. The inner *for* loop steps the variable *j* from the element after the one *i* points to through the end of the array. Inside the loops, the *i*th array element is compared against every remaining *j*th array element. If the *i*th element is out of sequence, it is swapped with the *j*th element. In short, the sort works by exhaustively comparing every element in the array against every other element until the array is in sequence. At each pass through the array by the outer loop, one more correct element "bubbles" to the top of the array, giving the sort its name.

If this sounds like an inefficient way to sort data, it is. Many C languages have a much faster and more efficient sorting function called *qsort()* (for quicksort) already in their libraries. Unfortunately, *qsort()* requires some techniques beyond the scope of this book. So our *sort()* function is provided as an easy-to-use replacement for it. If you have a *qsort()* in your library of C functions, feel free to replace *sort()* with it.

If you plan on writing a large number of data management programs, an improved sort routine is a must. In fact, you may need several different functions depending on your application.

After *recs* has been sorted, the function *writeout()* is called to rearrange the records in the checkbook. This function makes use of a trick; it knows that *delete()* "squishes" the records in the checkbook when one is deleted, moving up all the records after the one deleted to cover the hole produced by the deleted record. So, to rearrange the records, *writeout()* first copies each record in sorted order to the end of the checkbook with *insert()*, then deletes the old unsorted records from the beginning of the checkbook with *delete()*. As each old record is deleted, the new ones move up in the checkbook.

As you did with the *select()* function, be sure to add *sort()* to the list of *main()* options.

```
/* Listing 6-2. Checkbook Sorting Functions */

char *recs[100];        /* array of record addresses to sort */
int nrecs;
order()         /* sort checks in ascending order */
{
        readin();
        sort();
        writeout();
}


readin()        /* copy records to an array for sorting */
{
        int i;
        char *p;

        nrecs = 0;
        p = top;
        while (p < (_mend-1)) {
                recs[nrecs++] = p;
                p = p + strlen(p) + 1;
        }
}


writeout()      /* add the records back to memory in order */
{
        int i;
        char work[80];

        printf("\n");

        /* first, add copies to the end */
        for (i = 0; i < nrecs; i++) {
                printf("%s\n", recs[i]);
                insert(recs[i], _mend);
        }
```

```
        /* then delete the old records */
        for (i = 0; i < nrecs; i++) delete(top);
}
sort()              /* sort the array into ascending order */
{
        int i, j, pos;
        char *temp, num[80];

        printf("Starting position to sort by? ");
        gets(num, 80);
        if (strlen(num) == 0) return;
        pos = atoi(num)-1;
        for (i = 0; i < nrecs-1; i++) {
                for (j = i+1; j < nrecs; j++) {
                        if (strcmp(recs[i]+pos, recs[j]+pos) > 0) {
                                temp = recs[i];
                                recs[i] = recs[j];
                                recs[j] = temp;
                        }
                }
        }
}
```

SAMPLE RUN (ALPHABETICAL SORT)

```
A)dd, L)ist, D)elete, C)hange, O)rder, s(E)lect, S)ave, G)et,
e(X)it: a

Enter your data:

1 one
2 two
3 three

A)dd, L)ist, D)elete, C)hange, O)rder, s(E)lect, S)ave, G)et,
e(X)it: o
Starting position to sort by? 3

1 one
3 three
2 two

A)dd, L)ist, D)elete, C)hange, O)rder, s(E)lect, S)ave, G)et,
e(X)it:
```

Once again, this function executes slowly. This time, the delay is not due to the sort but to the *delete()* function, which is continually moving characters of memory around as the old unsorted records are deleted from the beginning of the checkbook.

A NAME AND PHONE FILE

You won't be learning any new statements or programming techniques in this section. Instead, you're going to use the program you've spent so much time developing in several other important business applications.

One of the mainstays in our office is (or was) a Rolodex file, a rotary gizmo that contains 3 x 5 cards with the names and phone numbers of people we call frequently. Now you are going to use the checkbook program to create an electronic Rolodex file for your customers' (or employees', or friends') names, addresses, and phone numbers. You can use the various features we've added to the program to find names, sort them, and build lists by various categories of customer.

Before you can begin, you need to decide on a format for your records. You need to store for each person:

- An ID number

- The name (last name first for sorting)

- A code telling whether the person is a friend, customer, etc.

- The phone number

- The address

The first field should be the ID number so that *find()* can locate the record. Remember that *find()* needs a number as the first field in the record so that it can locate specific records for changing and deleting. A sample record is shown below:

```
100 Franz,Marty 344-1183 :F:525 W. Walnut St, Kalamazoo MI 49071.
```

To make selecting easier, you can use these codes:

:F: for a friend

:C: for a customer

:B: for a business contact

:E: for an employee

NOTES

A uniform record layout is important. It makes it easier to detect errors and it ensures that the functions you write to manipulate the data—*sort()* and *select()*—will work properly.

The checkbook program you've written in C has several rules and restrictions. Your information must all be written in one continuous line with no carriage returns. (This is very important—*no carriage returns.*) The current checkbook program is limited to 80 characters of information per record. If you need more information, you can easily modify the add and change functions we developed earlier to accept more data. For example, if you need to have as many as 255 characters in some of your customer entries (so that you can keep track of past orders, preferences, etc.), go to the *add()* and *change()* functions, and wherever you see an 80, change it to 255.

Now you can begin to enter records into your file:

```
A)dd, L)ist, D)elete, C)hange, O)rder, s(E)lect, S)ave, G)et,
e(X)it: a

Enter your data:

1 Fuhrman, Lucy      :F: 387-2834
2 Farber, Audrey     :C: 594-3872    Smurfware, Inc.
3 Biolosky, Betty Jo :B: 281-2930    Targe Publishing Co.
4 Baker, Able        :E: 255-0983    East Sales Region
5 Crone, Parr        :E: 344-0277    Midwest Sales Region
6 Harris, Tom        :E: 986-2983    West Sales Region
7 Smlcznk, Fsgrn     :C: 483-8598    Alien Encounters Software

A)dd, L)ist, D)elete, C)hange, O)rder, s(E)lect, S)ave, G)et,
e(X)it: s
File name: names
Saving........
```

The information after the phone number is essentially free form. You can put in a company, a product description, a dollar sales value, a part number, or anything that makes your records easier to find and more useful. The names, however, are another story. Consistent with our record format, they must all begin in the same position and end in the same position. If the name is a short one, blanks must be added to the end to pad it to the full length. (An extra long name will be truncated, so plan ahead.) This trouble ensures that when a sort is performed, the people come out in the right order:

```
A)dd, L)ist, D)elete, C)hange, (O)rder, s(E)lect, S)ave, G)et,
e(X)it: o
Starting position to sort by? 4

4 Baker, Abel        :E: 255-0983    East Sales Region
3 Biolosky, Betty Jo :B: 281-2930    Targe Publishing Co.
5 Crone, Parr        :E: 344-0277    Midwest Sales Region
2 Farber, Audrey     :C: 594-3872    Smurfware, Inc.
1 Fuhrman, Lucy      :F: 387-2834
6 Harris, Tom        :E: 986-2983    West Sales Region
7 Smlcznk, Fsgrn     :C: 483-8598    Alien Encounters Software
```

If you needed a separate list of just your customers, you could use the program for that, too, with the select function:

```
A)dd, L)ist, D)elete, C)hange, O)rder, s(E)lect, S)ave, G)et,
e(X)it: s

Key to select: :C:

 2 Farber, Audrey    :C: 594-3872    Smurfware, Inc.
 7 Smlcznk, Fsgrn    :C: 483-8598    Alien Encounters Software
5 records deleted
```

As you can see, the program works well as a directory. If you need to find somebody's phone number, you can use the select function:

```
A)dd, L)ist, D)elete, C)hange, O)rder, s(E)lect, S)ave, G)et,
e(X)it: e
Key to select: Crone

 5 Crone, Parr       :E: 344-0277    Midwest Sales Region
6 records deleted
```

Or list everyone and pick out the name as you would from a phone directory:

```
A)dd, L)ist, D)elete, C)hange, O)rder, s(E)lect, S)ave, G)et,
e(X)it: 1
```

```
4 Baker, Abel           :E: 255-0983    East Sales Region
3 Biolosky, Betty Jo    :B: 281-2930    Targe Publishing Co.
5 Crone, Parr           :E: 344-0277    Midwest Sales Region
2 Farber, Audrey        :C: 594-3872    Smurfware, Inc.
1 Fuhrman, Lucy         :F: 387-2834
6 Harris, Tom           :E: 986-2983    West Sales Region
7 Smlcznk, Fsgrn        :C: 483-8598    Alien Encounters Software
```

Here are some other uses for the checkbook program:

- You can keep a "to do" list, organized by completion date and priority.

- You can keep track of business trip expenses for accounting purposes.

- You can organize your phone bill, sorting it by the time of call, the cost, or the number called.

- You can keep track of your business operating expenses, organizing them by department, account, or date.

- You can keep an inventory of home or office equipment for insurance purposes.

WHAT YOU LEARNED IN CHAPTER 6

We hope you now feel that all the programming you did in Chapter 4 was worthwhile. As you can see, the lowly checkbook program is actually a useful tool for many kinds of business record keeping.

In the next chapter, you'll be writing report programs that increase the utility of the checkbook program even more. These programs print mailing labels and a checkbook register. With these tools in hand, you can finally get that balance out of the checkbook program. In the process, you'll be learning more about C's file input/output and system functions.

The new C concepts and functions you learned in this chapter are:

pointer expressions and unary *

nested *for* and *while* loops

strcmp() and *strcpy()* functions

decrement (— —) operator

==

The Bottom Line: Formatting Reports
7

Accurate, useful reports are the most important part of any business software system. Although all your company's data may be safely organized and maintained on your computer, unless you can obtain useful reports in a timely manner, the system is nearly worthless. In this chapter, you learn how to write report programs in C. You won't need to learn new C functions or programming techniques. Instead, you put what you've learned in previous chapters to work as you create report "modules" for use with your new, improved checkbook program and, for the first time, get a hard copy of your results.

A GENERAL REPORT PROGRAM

Most report programs have a similar structure despite the widely varying reports they produce. They usually read a file of data, print items from each record in the file, and provide a report summary at the end of the file. Before we go on to examine this structure in more detail, here's a glossary of some new terms we'll be using:

title	The report name, preparer name, company name, program name, page number, etc. that appear at the top of each page.

headings	The names of the fields, displayed column by column just above the first line of detail.
detail	The individual fields, displayed in tabular format with each line in the table corresponding to a single record.
summary	Totals and percentages that appear at the end of the report.
page break	The start of a new page when the current one is full or one of the individual fields changes value.

With these terms in mind, let's look at a generic report program. The *main()* function, written in English, looks like this:

```
while not done yet
    ask for data file name
    if none, break
    open data file
    start at line 1, page 1
    clear summary totals
    open printer file
    print titles and headings
    generate report
    close printer file
    close data file
repeat
```

To forestall complications, two separate files are used: a *data file*, which is read by the report program and contains the records to report on, and a *printer file*, which contains the output report.

We need to write several new functions, the most obvious of which are "print titles and headings" and "generate reports."

The first function, "print titles and headings," centers the text, prints headings for the detail columns, and keeps track of how many pages have been printed. Exactly what this function will do in each case will depend on what you and your company like to see on reports. For example, you might want your company's name and address, the date, and the program name to be printed in the heading.

The second function, "generate report," is more complicated. It can be described as follows:

```
while still records in data file
      read data file
      skip to next line
      if at end of page {
            print titles and headings
      }
      print fields needed in detail
      calculate fields needed in summary
repeat
```

It's up to your report program to make sure that all the pages contain an equal number of lines and that a proper title and heading appear at the top of each page. To accomplish these goals, your program needs to keep track of both the lines printed on the current page and the number of pages that have already been printed.

For $8\frac{1}{2}$-by-11-inch paper, there are 66 lines on a page. Allowing for three-line margins at the top and bottom of the page, this usually means 60 lines of actual output can fit comfortably on each report page (see Figure 7-1). To keep track of how many lines have been printed on the current page, a counter is incremented each time a detail or heading line of text is printed. When the count reaches 60, a new page is started, the titles and headings are printed at the top, the page count is incremented, and the line count is reset. This procedure is repeated until there are no more detailed items to print. Since this is quite a lot of programming, it looks as though there should be a separate function for this counting procedure:

```
increment line count
if line count is more than 60 {
      print titles and headings
      line count = 0
}
print newline
```

We now have a basic program structure with which to produce reports. In the next few sections, you develop the functions that are common to all the report programs in the chapter and write three distinct report modules to produce the detail and summary information needed for each report. But before we can start writing these functions, we need to know how to work with printers in C.

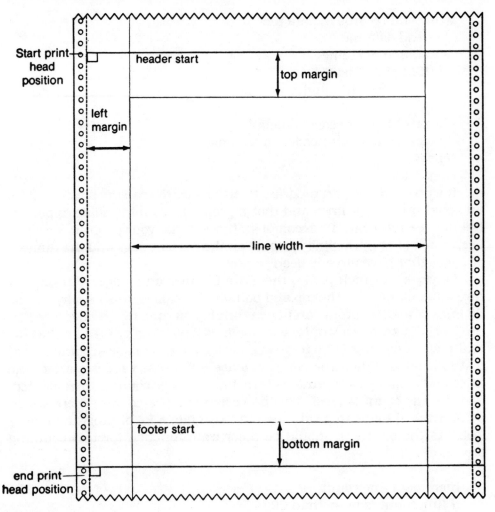

FIG. 7-1

USING YOUR PRINTER

One of the most important features of the C programming language, as you've come to appreciate throughout this book, is that the language statements are very simple. This simplicity results from the use of functions. With the aid of a standard C library of functions, you can do advanced math [*pow()*, *sqrt()*], string handling [*strlen()*, *strcpy()*], and file input and output [*fprintf()*, *fgets()*]. You don't need special language statements to do any of these things in your program because the library provides these facilities for you.

In providing file input/output functions, C designers were careful to make the functions *fopen()*, *fclose()*, *fgets()*, and *fprintf()* all device independent. That is, these functions don't care whether the file you want to read from or write to is on a diskette, a hard disk, a printer, a magnetic tape, or a device that hasn't been invented yet. The computer's operating system is assumed to take care of the hardware device assignment for you. This approach is in contrast to that of programming languages like BASIC, in which you use one statement (PRINT) to send output to your screen and another (LPRINT) to send text to the printer.

The practical result is that you can open your computer's printer in C just as you would any other file, by following the procedure you learned in Chapter 4, page 82. (But don't try to read from your printer; it's a write-only device.) Each version of C uses a different file name for the printer. With Computer Innovation's C on the IBM PC, the printer filename is called "prn:." With Aztec C on the Apple][, the printer filename is "pr:." And on Unix, the printer may have a name such as "/dev/lpr." Check in your C language manual for specifics.

Once you've opened the printer under the correct name, you can print to it using the *fprintf()* function. To send a formfeed to a printer, write:

```
unsigned printer;

printer = fopen("lpt1:", "w");

fprintf(printer, "%c", '\f');
```

The instructions you need to obtain other special effects (e.g., underline or boldface) will vary from printer to printer. As you get more experienced, you may want to write a set of functions that make full use of your printer's special effects, such as alternate character sets or compressed and enhanced printing modes, and put them in your own C library for repeated use.

GENERIC REPORT FUNCTIONS

DESCRIPTION

This section presents a *main()* function for a generic report program, plus some additional smaller functions. These functions will be tested in the next section, when you add a reporting module for printing mailing labels.

HOW IT WORKS

The *main()* function sets up the global variables used by all other functions in the program, including page count, line count, and number of lines on a page. It uses the function *getfile()* developed back in Chapter 5, page 91, to get the name of the file it is to process. If the user presses RETURN without entering a file name, the program terminates. Otherwise, the file is opened and the file descriptor is returned.

After the data file is opened, the printer file is opened by the function *openprt()*. (It's up to the individual user to be sure the printer is turned on and functioning properly before the program starts, for if an error occurs after the program has begun, the program terminates.) As a means of forestalling possible conflicts, the printer's file descriptor is a global variable (printer) rather than local to *main()*.

Once the files are open, a new page is started and *detail()* is called. Different report programs will have different *detail()* functions (that is, the statements within the function will differ), depending on what you want the function to do. The *detail()* function processes each record in the data file and prints a detail line for it. After the last record in the data file has been read, *detail()* returns to *main()*, and *summary()* is called. As with *detail()*, a separate *summary()* function is required for each of your reports. The *summary()* function produces any summary information (totals, etc.) you require at the end of the report. After *summary()*, both the data file and printer file are closed and the whole process can be repeated for a new data set or report.

The functions *newline()* and *newpage()* control lines and pagination. Use *newline()* everywhere in your report that you need to print a new line ('\n'); this function will automatically count the lines and start a new page if the line count for the current page has been exceeded. You should also add any statements that print titles and headings into *newpage()* to be sure they will appear each time a new page is printed. Note that a form-feed is not printed at the top of the first page; this permits the user to align the form in the printer before running the program.

For future reference, the global variables that control lines and pages are:

lines	counts lines on the page
page	holds the current page number
pagecount	holds number of lines/page

Franz & Good: Writing Business Programs in C Language (Chilton)

LISTING

```
/* Listing 7-1. Generic Report Program
   Includes functions:
   openprt()    open printer for output
   newpage()    start a new page
   newline()    print newline, keep count of lines
*/

unsigned printer;                     /* printer file descriptor */
int lines;                            /* line on page */
int page;                             /* current page number */
int pagecount;                        /* number lines/page */

main()
{
        int quit;
        unsigned fd;

        page = 0;
        pagecount = 60;
        while (1 == 1) {
                fd = getfile();
                if (fd == 0) break;
                openprt();
                newpage();
                detail(fd);
                summary();
                fclose(fd);
                fclose(printer);
        }
}

openprt()          /* open printer file for output */
{
        printer = fopen("lpt1:", "w");
        if (printer == 0) {
                printf("\n\nCan't open printer for report\n");
                exit(0);
        }
}
```

```
newline()        /* print newline and keep count of lines */
{
        if (lines++ > pagecount) newpage();
        fprintf(printer, "\n");
}
newpage()        /* start a new page, reset counts */
{
        if (page != 0) fprintf(printer, "%c", '\f');
        page++;
        lines = 0;

        /* print your titles and headings here */
}
```

PRINTING MAILING LABELS

DESCRIPTION

Now you can put your generic report functions to work. In this section, you write a program to create mailing labels from a name and address file. To test the program, you can use one of the files you've created with the record-keeping program you developed in Chapters 4, 5, and 6.

Before you can write the *detail()* function, you need to establish a record layout for each name and address. The layout should start with the person's name (last name first, padded with blanks for correct sorting), followed by the address. To generate a mailing label, use a backslash (\) everywhere you want a new line on the label. Why? Recall in Chapter 3, you wrote a function called *label()* to format a character string containing backslashes as a mailing label. If you format your records with these slashes, you can use this function. Here's what a name and address record might look like:

```
52 Franz, Marty \525 W. Walnut\Kalamazoo MI 49007
```

And here's how it would appear as a mailing label:

```
52 Franz, Marty
525 W. Walnut St.
Kalamazoo MI 49007
```

For this report, all you need to write is a *detail()* function, since no summary information is required. Be sure you convert the call to *summary()*

V

Bugstopper's Notebook: Using "Magic Numbers"

Experience teaches us that nothing changes more often than what we expect to be permanent. To simplify the inevitable adjustments, experienced programmers try to express constants like 60 lines/page as variables whenever possible. In our report program, the number of lines per page is kept in a global variable *(pagecount)*. As a result, when you need to modify this number (when printing mailing labels for example), you don't have to make the change every place it appears in the program; you have to change only the single assignment statement

pagecount = 60

in *main()*. Be sure to use such "magic numbers" in your programs, too.

in *main()* to a comment using /* */, or write a dummy *summary()* function so you won't get an error (we did this in the listing that follows).

HOW IT WORKS

The *detail()* function uses *gets()* to read the name and address record from the data file, and then calls *label()* to print the label. The function *label()* has been altered to go to the printer using *fprintf()* instead of to the terminal with *printf()*, but otherwise it is the same as in Chapter 4.

LISTING

```
/* Listing 7-2. Mailing Labels Functions
   Includes functions:
   label()     print string in label format
   detail()    read file and print labels
   summary()   dummy function for now
*/

label(s)                 /* format string s as a mailing label */
char s[];
{
        int i;

        fprintf(printer, "\n");
        for (i = 0; i < strlen(s); i++) {
                if (s[i] == '\\')
                        fprintf(printer, "\n");
                else
                        fprintf(printer, "%c", s[i]);
        }
        fprintf(printer, "\n\n");        /* finish with newlines */
}

detail(fd)
unsigned fd;
{
        int c, i;
        char s[80];
```

```
        printf("\nReading");
        while (fgets(s, 80, fd) != 0) {
                printf(".")
                label(s);
                }
        printf("\n");
}
summary()        \* not needed yet *\
{
}
```

SAMPLE RUN

To run this program, you first need to create a test file of labels using the record-keeping program:

```
A)dd, L)ist, D)elete, C)hange, O)rder, s(E)lect, S)ave, G)et,
e(X)it: a

Enter your data:

1 Franz, Marty    \525 W. Walnut\Kalamazoo MI 49007
2 Good, Phil      \1036 Paw Paw Lake Drive\Elkhardt IN 49371

A)dd, L)ist, D)elete, C)hange, O)rder, s(E)lect, S)ave, G)et,
e(X)it: s
File name: labels.dat
Saving..

A)dd, L)ist, D)elete, C)hange, O)rder, s(E)lect, S)ave, G)et,
e(X)it: x
```

Now that the test data file has been created, you can run the mailing label program to print sample labels:

```
Print Mailing Labels

File name: labels.dat
Reading..

Done
Hit any key to continue...
```

The labels will be printed on your printer:

```
1 Franz, Marty
525 W. Walnut
Kalamazoo MI 49007

2 Good, Phil
1036 Paw Paw Lake Drive
Elkhardt IN 49371
```

NOTES

You can, and should, write a program to omit the leading sequence number from the label by modifying the *detail()* function. (*Hint:* Use the *sscanf()* function, or write a function of your own to scan the string character-by-character.) And you may want to reverse the order in which the first and last names are given. (*Hint:* Write a function to scan the name string until you reach the comma that separates the names, then use *strcpy()*, *strncpy()* as described in Chapter 6.)

Here are two more ways to increase your productivity. To reach a select audience or to save with bulk mail postage, use the record-keeping program to sort the list before you print the labels. To make it easier to check the forms' alignment for correct printing, include a "test label" made of all *x*'s at the start of each run.

PRINTING A FORMATTED CHECK REGISTER

A hard copy of your electronic checkbook is a must when you sit down with your partners or your CPA. The next program you develop reads a data file containing check information and prints a check register. The register shows the check number, the amount of the check (or deposit), the date written, the date cashed (since this is the data printed on your bank statement), and a description of the check. A sample check in the checkbook file might look like this:

```
301 64.65 10/01/84 10/10/84 Dan Brown — cat bite
```

The program below lists the checks and computes a running balance. Deposits are entered into the checkbook as negative amounts; this simplifies the calculations; the amount on the check can be subtracted from the balance whether it is a check or a deposit.

HOW IT WORKS

In this version of *detail()*, the *sscanf()* function is used to extract each of the fields from the check records. The *sscanf()* function scans the record string and fills the variable *n* with the check number, *amount* with the amount of the check, *writ* with a string containing the date the check was written, and *cash* with a string containing the date the check was cashed. Only the variable *amount* is really processed. It is subtracted from *balance*, the account balance entered when the data file is first opened (notice that *main()* has been modified to reflect this change). The other variables filled by *sscanf()*, *n*, *writ*, and *cash* are simply copied to the output line.

There is no clever way to align the fields in their output columns. We used a sheet of graph paper to design the report below and spent what seemed an interminable length of time in counting out the little boxes. But the completed output was correct the first time the program was run.

LISTING

```
/* Listing 7-3. Check Register Program Version 1 */

int lines;                  /* line on page */
int page;                   /* current page number */
int pagecount;              /* number of lines/page */
unsigned printer;

float balance;              /* current balance */
char regtitle[81];          /* check register title line */

main()
{

        int quit;
        unsigned fd;
```

```
            page = 0;
            pagecount = 60;
            fill(regtitle, 80, ' ');
            center(regtitle, "Checkbook Register #1");
            while (1 == 1) {
                    fd = getfile();
                    if (fd == 0) break;
                    openprt();
                    newpage();
                    printf("Starting balance");
                    balance = gf();
                    detail(fd);
                    summary();
                    fclose(fd);
                    fclose(printer);
            }
}

newpage()        /* start a new page, reset counts */
{

        if (page != 0) fprintf(printer, "%c", '\f');
        page++;
        lines = 0;

        /* print your titles and headings here */
        newline();
        newline();
        fprintf(printer, regtitle);
        newline();
        newline();
        fprint(printer,
            "Check   Date      Date                        Check");
        newline();
        fprintf(printer,
            " No.   Written   Cashed      Description Amount   Balance");
        newline();
        newline();
}
detail(fd)
unsigned fd;
{
        int c, i, n;
        float amount;
        char s[80], writ[9], cash[9], desc[80];
```

Franz & Good: Writing Business Programs in C Language (Chilton)

```
                printf("\nReading");
                while (fgets(s, 80, fd) != 0) {
                        s[strlen(s)-1] = '\0';
                        sscanf(s, "%d %f %8s %8s", &n, &amount, writ, cash);
                        strcpy(desc, s+29);
                        balance = balance - amount;
                        fprintf(printer, " %3d    %-8s %-8s %-20s %7.2f %7.2f",
                                n, writ, cash, desc, amount, balance);
                        newline();
                        printf(".");
                }
                printf("\n");
}
```

SAMPLE RUN

To run this program, you first need to create a test file containing a few
of your checks. You also have to balance your checkbook (sorry) so you
can check the program's balance against what the bank says you have in
your account. Your report should look like this:

```
                          Checkbook Register #1

Check    Date      Date                            Check
No.      Written   Cashed    Description           Amount   Balance

100      10/01/84  10/15/84  Test Check #1          10.00   -10.00
101      10/01/84  10/15/84  Test Check #2          20.00   -30.00
102      10/01/84  -         Test Deposit #1       -30.00     0.00
```

A BETTER CHECK REGISTER

DESCRIPTION

You've been patient with us so far as we developed an electronic checkbook that would first record, then select, and finally print a register of
your checks and deposits. As a bonus for completing all your fundamental C programming requirements, you're going to learn an additional
function that can actually save you a hundred dollars or more each year
(at least as long as interest rates stay up).

The "float" on a particular check is the amount of time that elapses
between when you wrote the check and when the recipient presented it

to the bank for deposit. If you write a lot of checks for a lot of money, you can use this float time to your advantage by depositing the money in short-term investments. (Bear in mind that this is *not* what the banks consider float—the recipient's bank probably holds the check up to five days more for reasons of its own.) The "float" field will be added to the right of the other fields on the previous report.

HOW IT WORKS

A new function, *mdys()*, converts a string in the mm/dd/yy format to three floating-point variables containing the month, day, and year. We use one of the functions you created in Chapter 2, *julmdy()*, to convert these variables in turn into a Julian date. A new function, *diff()*, computes the difference between two Julian dates and returns the difference in the form of an integer. It's a more straightforward routine than the one we wrote in Chapter 2 (page 27) because it takes advantage of the pointer variables that were introduced in Chapter 6. Notice the *if* statement in *diff()* that ensures that the conversion to Julian is attempted *only if* there's a valid date in both *date1* or *date2*. If one or the other date was not converted properly, the difference is set to zero and the function returns.

A working *summary()* function has also been added to this report. This prints the number of checks processed and their total, and the number of deposits processed and their total. The global variables *nchecks*, *ndeposits*, *tchecks*, and *tdeposits* keep track of these summary figures.

LISTING

```
/* Listing 7-4. Check Register Program Version 2 */

int lines;              /* line on page */
int page;               /* current page number */
int pagecount;          /* number lines/page */
unsigned printer;

float balance;          /* current balance */
char regtitle[81];      /* check register title line */
int nchecks, ndeposits; /* number of checks and deposits */
float tchecks, tdeposits; /* total of checks and deposits */
```

```
main()
{
        int quit;
        unsigned fd;

        page = 0;
        pagecount = 60;
        fill(regtitle, 80, ' ');
        center(regtitle, "Checkbook Register #2");
        while (1 == 1) {
                fd = getfile();
                if (fd == 0) break;
                openprt();
                newpage();
                printf("Starting balance");
                balance = gf();
                detail(fd);
                summary();
                fclose(fd);
                fclose(printer);
        }
}


newpage()          /* start a new page, reset counts */
{
        if (page != 0) fprintf(printer, "%c", '\f');
        page++;
        lines = 0;

        /* print your titles and headings here */
        newline();
        newline();
        fprintf(printer, regtitle);
        newline();
        newline();
        fprintf(printer, "Check   Date        Date                         ");
        fprintf("Check           Float");
        newline();
        fprintf(printer, " No.  Written   Cashed    Description  ");
        fprintf("   Amount Balance Days");
        newline();
        newline();
}
```

```
detail(fd)
unsigned fd;
{
        int c, i, n, days;
        float amount;
        char s[80], writ[9], cash[9], desc[80];

        printf("\nReading");
        while (fgets(s, 80, fd) != 0) {
                s[strlen(s)-1] = '\0';
                sscanf(s, "%d %f %8s %8s", &n, &amount, writ, cash);
                strcpy(desc, s+29);
                balance = balance - amount;
                if (amount < 0) {
                        ndeposits++;
                        tdeposits = tdeposits - amount;
                }
                else {
                        nchecks++;
                        tchecks = tchecks + amount;
                }
                days = diff(writ, cash);
                fprintf(printer,
                        " %3d   %-8s   %-8s   %-20s   %7.2f   %7.2f     %2d",
                            n,   writ, cash, desc, amount, balance, days);
                newline();
                printf(".");
        }
        printf("\n");
}

summary()
{
        newline();
        newline();
        fprintf(printer,
                "Number of checks:    %2d for %7.2f", nchecks,
                    tchecks);
        newline();
        fprintf(printer,
                "Number of deposits:    %2d for %7.2f", ndeposits,
                    tdeposits);
        newline();
        fprintf(printer, "%c", '\f');
}
```

```
diff(date1, date2)
char date1[], date2[];
{
        int di;
        float m, d, y, jul1, jul2;
        mdys(&m, &d, &y, date1);
        jul1 = julmdy(m, d, y);
        if (strlen(date2) == 8) {
                mdys(&m, &d, &y, date2);
                jul2 = julmdy(m, d, y);
                di = jul2 - jul1;
                if (di < 0) di = -di;
        }
        else di =0;
        return di;
}


mdys(m, d, y, s)
float *m, *d, *y;
char *s;
{
        *m = atof(s);
        *d = atof(s + 3);
        *y = atof(s + 6);
}
```

SAMPLE RUN

You can use the same test file you used in the last section for this program. Your revised report should look like this:

Checkbook Register #2

Check No.	Date Written	Date Cashed	Description	Check Amount	Balance	Float Days
100	10/01/84	10/15/84	Test Check #1	10.00	-10.00	15
101	10/01/84	10/15/84	Test Check #2	20.00	-30.00	15
102	10/01/84	-	Test Deposit #1	-30.00	0.00	0

```
Number of checks:    2 for    30.00
Number of deposits:  1 for    30.00
```

DESIGN YOUR OWN REPORTS

The report structure presented in this chapter is easily adapted to a variety of reporting needs. For example, you could modify the checkbook register to print negative amounts and balances enclosed in parentheses or with dollar signs in front of them. (*Hint:* You will have to print each detail line field-by-field instead of with a single *fprintf()* function. This means more programming but provides you with greater flexibility. For example, you could put deposits and checks in separate columns like a ledger sheet to make the register easier to read.)

Another profitable approach is to develop a single, general-purpose program similar in concept to the general-purpose record-keeping program you developed in Chapter 7. Each time this new program was executed, it would read in the types and lengths of the fields that were to be printed, the titles, and the heading names for each individual report. It would then "create" the report from these specifications. [*Hint:* Build format strings for *sscanf()* and *fprintf()* in *detail()*. Use the *strcpy()* and *strcat()* functions.]

WHAT YOU LEARNED IN CHAPTER 7

In this chapter, you developed a standard program for generating tabular reports. You learned how to customize this program for specific applications and how to produce printed copies of your reports. In writing your report programs, you used many of the functions you had developed in earlier chapters including *julmdy()* from Chapter 2, and *fill()*, *center()*, and *label()* from Chapter 3. This shows us once again how useful functions are in the development of C programs. Care taken in writing small, general-purpose C functions will pay you back time and time again.

=================================

Writing Your Own C Programs 8

You've come a long way from Chapter 1, when you worked with your first C program. By now you should feel comfortable with the C statements and functions presented in this book. In this chapter, you learn about the range of software applications for C and about C toolkits and libraries that can simplify your programming tasks.

ADVANCED PROGRAMMING CONCEPTS

C is a complex language. Although you've gained insight into the more common statements and functions, you've really only scratched the surface of C's potential. In this section, you catch a glimpse of what's ahead for you to learn in the C language. These are advanced features you might or might not need depending on the kind of programming you do.

POINTERS AND STRUCTURES

Pointers (described in Chapter 6) are extremely important in C. In this book, they were used interchangeably with strings in many of your programs. But in advanced C programming, pointers have many more functions.

To begin with, you can use a pointer to represent an array element. This makes it possible for you to do complex array arithmetic without resorting to often-confusing brackets. Second, you can use arrays of pointers to save space when sorting or processing strings. This was done in the *sort()* function in Chapter 6. In short, you can use pointers to represent larger variables in memory in your programs, saving a lot of processing time.

Another, more important use of pointers is in conjunction with *structures*. Like arrays, structures are a group of memory locations allocated and accessed under a single name. Unlike arrays, in which all the memory locations must be of the same type (e.g., *int, unsigned, float,* or *char*), structures can contain several different types of variables. For example, suppose you wanted to create a single payroll variable that contained a person's name (*char*), ID number (*int*), and pay rate (*float*). You could do this using a structure with the following statement:

```
struct pay {
    int id;
    char name[50];
    float payrate;
} payrec;
```

Don't worry about the syntax of everything you see in this example—it is explained in more advanced texts, such as *The C Programming Language* by Bryan W. Kernighan and Dennis M. Ritchie (John Wiley & Sons, 1978). For now, you should know that this statement creates a variable called *payrec* that has inside it three other variables, *id, name,* and *payrate.* You can either treat these variables as a unit, under the name *payrec,* or refer to each variable separately. For example,

```
payrec.id = 10;
strcpy(payrec.name, "Phil Good");
payrec.payrate = 10.00;
```

You can even declare pointers to structures and pass entire structures between functions using them. Structures constitute a powerful way to organize your variables when you do complex programming. You should use structures whenever you find you have a group of variables that together represent a single "object" of data in your program.

#DEFINE AND #INCLUDE

Another powerful feature of many C dialects is the *preprocessor*. This is a module of the compiler that scans your program before it is actually compiled into code. The preprocessor allows you to "program your programs" using statements such as *#include* and *#define.* The first statement, *#include,* directs the preprocessor to start reading statements from another source file. This allows you to place commonly used variable declarations, program titles, etc. in a single file accessible to all your programs. When you want to change these common statements, you have to change only a single file, not each program that uses the statements. A common *#include* statement you'll see in many C programs is

```
#include "stdio.h"
```

In most C compilers, the file *stdio.h* contains the declarations needed for file input and output, including standard file descriptors and error messages.

The second preprocessor statement mentioned above, *#define,* assigns one symbol to another. This is more easily seen than explained. For example, you've often used the constant 80 to stand for the largest line your program will read from the keyboard. You could use *#define* to assign MAXLINE to 80 instead, like this:

```
#define MAXLINE 80
```

And then everywhere you use 80, as in

```
char buf[80];
gets(buf, 80);
```

change it to

```
char buf[MAXLINE];
gets(buf, MAXLINE);
```

Why go through this trouble? Because later, when you want to increase the line size to 255 characters, you only need to change a single statement, namely

```
#define MAXLINE 255
```

Franz & Good: Writing Business Programs in C Language (Chilton)

All the other statements that reference MAXLINE in your program will be changed automatically by the preprocessor. This allows you to conveniently use and manage "magic numbers" in your C-language programs.

You should use #*define* and #*include* together when you are working on large software systems made up of many programs so that you can place all common systemwide "magic numbers" in a single place for easier maintenance.

TYPEDEFS

Still another powerful feature in C is a statement called *typedef.* This allows you to create your own data type names to represent structures and arrays in your programs. Using the example structure defined earlier, you could create a *typedef* called *payptr* that declares a pointer to that structure:

```
typedef struct pay *PAYPTR;
```

You can now declare pointers to the pay structure with

```
PAYPTR p;
```

instead of

```
struct pay *p;
```

Use *typedef* statements to make your large programs more readable and to "hide" the internal structure of key variables.

All the C features presented above—structures, preprocessor commands, and *typedef* statements—are really most useful to you when you are writing large, complex programs. For small programs or extremely limited applications (such as ROM programs in single-board microprocessors), you don't really need these features (C purists, of course, will disagree).

INTERPRETERS

Throughout this book, the word *compiler* has been used to mean any program that translates the C language on your computer. Actually, there are two very different ways to use the C programming language. The first is with a program called an *interpreter* and the second is with a program called a *compiler*. In this section and the one that follows, you will learn about the relative advantages of each when writing programs. (More on this subject is contained in Appendix I.)

An interpreter translates and executes your program line-by-line. It takes only a few seconds from the time you've written your program with the interpreter until the results appear on the screen. No separate object module is produced, and additional time-consuming compilation and linking are unnecessary. On most microcomputers the BASIC language is interpreted: you edit your program and type RUN to execute it.

The advantages of interpreters are:

- Easy operation (one step between edit and run)
- Faster development time
- Easier debugging

Because they execute your programs a line at a time, interpreters can stop your program when it reaches a particular line so that you can look at variables, check memory, etc. This ability to stop the program allows for efficient debugging and makes interpreters very popular.

The disadvantages of using an interpeter are:

- Much slower program execution (5 to 25 times slower)
- May not support full C language
- Additional libraries not present
- More memory needed for development

The first of these handicaps is readily overcome by using an interpreter to develop and debug your programs and a compiler to produce the final executable version.

Introducing C is a comprehensive C interpreter available from
Computer Innovations, Inc.
980 Shrewsbury Ave., Suite 301
Tinton Falls, NJ 07724
(201 542-5920).

It will let you develop a wide variety of business applications, and it comes with an extensive library of C utility functions, including graphics. Introducing C is upward compatible with the C-86 compiler described later in this chapter. This means that any program you develop with Introducing

C will run without modification when compiled by C-86. As a result, many software developers use Introducing C to write and debug their programs initially and then compile them for faster execution using C-86.

Instant C for the IBM PC features a full-screen editor and one-step operation, support for the full C programming language, the ability to set variables and execute single functions and expressions, and a standard library. It can also generate object modules that will occupy less memory and execute faster than the original interpreted version of your program. It is available from

Rational Systems, Inc.
P.O. Box 480
Natlick, MA 01760
(617 653-6194)

Another interpreter, tiny-c, was a first attempt by the author of Introducing C. At the time of this writing, it is the only interpreter that runs on 8-bit CP/M-based computers like the Kaypro and the Quay. The manual is excellent, but the product lacks online prompts and can be baffling. It supports a nonstandard version of the language, too. It is available from

tiny c associates
P.O. Box 269
Holmdel, NJ 07733
(201 671-2296)

COMPILERS

A compiler is a program that translates your C program into a machine-language program. The input C program is called the *source program* and the output machine-language program is called the *object module*. A process called *linking* is required to turn the object module into a program that will execute on your computer.

You should use a compiler in your C programming mainly for performance reasons. A C program processed by a compiler will run faster than one processed by an interpreter. Some other advantages of a compiler, which may or may not be important to you, are:

- Full support of C-language standard

- Faster program execution

- Assembler language output available

- ROM-able object code output available

A couple of the disadvantages to using a compiler for your programs are:

- Slower development time
- More difficulty debugging programs

It takes four steps to compile a program. You create and edit your program using a text editor, compile it, link it, and, finally, run it. If you make a mistake, you have to repeat this process as often as needed until the program works. This can be very time-consuming.

Debugging programs is more difficult with a compiler because the list and trace facilities available with an interpreter aren't present. You have to insert extra *printf()* statements where you think the problem is and use their output to determine what's wrong.

Recently, some compilers have included a *source-level debugger*. This feature automatically places extra *printf()* statements into your code for you, giving you the functions called, line numbers, etc. so that you have more information to work with when debugging your programs.

An experienced programmer doesn't really need the improved debugging faciliities of the interpreter once a standard library of commonly used functions has been developed and tested. However, an interpreter is invaluable to a beginner who is learning C.

C COMPILER CHECKLIST

This section contains a checklist you can use when purhasing a compiler (or interpreter). The main features to evaluate in a C compiler are portability, the extent of its library, the performance of both the compiler and the programs it generates, and the overall usability of the product.

PORTABILITY

Portability really means adherence to the C-language standard as described in *The C Programming Language*. Without adherence to this language standard, you can't transfer programs between different computer systems or other C-language products. Some language features such as floating-point numbers, structures, and *typedef* statements are often omitted from C compilers on CP/M and the Apple][. They may not all be important to you, depending on your applications. At a minimum, the compiler or interpreter you choose should support standard C-language syntax (if not all the statements) and introduce no nonstandard statements of its own.

- Supports full C standard?
    - Floating point?
    - Structures?
    - *Typedef?*
- Standard I/O library?

LIBRARY

All compilers come with a library of standard functions for the convenience of the programmer. This library must include the standard I/O functions like *fopen()* and *fgets()*. Otherwise, you will have problems when you attempt to transfer your programs from one model of computer to another. The *read()*, *write()*, and *lseek()* functions are essential if you're going to work with random-access files in advanced data management and accounting systems. The *exec()* function lets you "chain" your programs together so one can call another. It will let you build easy-to-use applications software that takes advantage of menus. Features like floating-point hardware support, extra operating system functions, and an assembler interface may also be important to you if you want to write software products in C. An assembler interface to the library would let you replace library routines with assembly-language versions for better performance.

- *Read(), write(), lseek()* available?
- *exec()* available?
- Floating-point hardware supported?
- Extra operating system functions?
- Source code available?
- Interface to assembler?

PERFORMANCE

The ideal compiler will have four properties:

It will compile programs quickly, minimizing delays during development.

It will compile them tightly, so that a minimum of memory is required for their execution.

It will produce code that executes quickly.

Its library of C functions will be portable so you can easily transfer the programs you write from computer to computer.

Unfortunately, such an ideal is difficult to achieve in practice, and compromise is almost inevitable. For example, you might have to trade off execution speed and program size for portability. (In this case, one solution would be to break your programs into smaller pieces called *overlays* that you keep on disk or diskette and bring in one at a time as needed.)

- Fast compilation?
- Fast execution?
- Small object-code size?
- ROM-able object code?
- Relocatable object code?
- Overlays supported?

USABILITY

Usability refers to how easy it is to use the various programs in the software package. You need an editor for most C compilers, and some packages provide one. If not, one will have to be purchased separately, adding to your cost and learning time. Some compilers allow you to save many small source files in one large one through a source librarian program. This saves on diskette space and file handling. The ability to compile several programs with one command can be valuable if you're working on large programming projects. The type of linker the package uses can also be important. If the one that comes with your operating system is used, it means you can link your C programs with those written in compiled BASIC, FORTRAN, or COBOL.

Finally, you should examine the user's manual. The lack of an index may indicate that the program's authors don't consider their manual to be worth your reference. An index is a must. And insist on an alphabetized listing of all functions in the library—you'll refer to it often.

- Editor provided?
- Source librarian provided?

- Multiple compilations allowed?
- Standard linker user?
- User manual with index, function list?

POPULAR COMPILERS

UNIX AND XENIX

The Unix operating system (and its compatible variants like Xenix from Microsoft) comes with a C compiler and its associated programming tools standard. These tools include the compiler itself, several program editors, a linker, terminal libraries, and a program called "lint" that checks your programs for bits of fluff (portability problems). The compiler meets (in fact, it defines) the standard described in *The C Programming Language*. This is the most complete C programming environment available.

MS-DOS

This operating system runs on many popular microcomputers, including the IBM PC, Compaq, Televideo PC, AT&T, and others. No C compiler is standard with the system. A program editor and linker are provided with it, however. Among the more popular compilers available for use with MS-DOS are Lattice C, C-86, and C-Ware C.

Lattice C enjoys a complete library and full compliance with the C-language standard. It is available from several distributors, including Microsoft and Lifeboat Associates, and it enjoys excellent support. Recent benchmark tests showed that it consistently produced the fastest and shortest programs. If it lacks anything, it is extended library functions, and this can be remedied by purchasing an add-on library from Lattice called the C Food Smorgasbord, which contains some of these extra functions. This product is available from

Lattice, Inc.
P.O. Box 648
Hoffman Estates, IL 60195
(312 843-2405)

Computer Innovations C-86 C is another complete C compiler. It features an extended library with graphics, terminal support, and access to MS-DOS functions, plus a lower price than Lattice C. Like Lattice, however, C-86 C also enjoys excellent developer support, including a hot line and bulletin board system. It is available from

Computer Innovations, Inc.
980 Shrewsbury Ave., Suite 310
Tinton Falls, NJ 07724
(201 542-5920)

C-Ware C is a complete C development system including a full-screen editor, assembler, and linker. It features an attractive price, fast compilation, and a number of large C programs in source form for you to study and learn from. It is available from
C-Ware
1607 New Brunswick Ave.
Sunnyvale, CA 94087
(408 736-6905)

Whitesmith's is another C compiler for the MS-DOS environment. Whitesmith's compilers are professional-quality, full C-language implementations. The compilers can be difficult to use for beginners, since an assembly step is required after compilation. A unique feature of Whitesmith's is the availability of cross-compilers. These let you develop your programs on a larger computer (such as PDP-11 or VAX) and produce object code that is loaded and run on a smaller computer (such as an IBM PC or CP/M system). If you are interested in this kind of development environment, with large-system programming tools and multiple user capabilities, then this compiler is recommended. Order from
Whitesmith's, Ltd.
97 Lowell Road
Concord, MA 01742
(617 369-8499)

CP/M

CP/M is a popular operating system on many 8-bit microcomputers. There are several C compilers available for it, though certainly not as many as for the exploding MS-DOS market. Since many CP/M systems are used in process-control and lab-automation applications, you might be more interested in being able to get assembler language or ROM-able code than in portability.

BDS C is an established, reliable product that has excellent developer support, fast compilation, efficient object code, and a good manual. Its biggest drawback is that it is nonstandard in its language support (lacking *float* variables, for example). Still, BDS C is an excellent product for nonportable applications. It can be ordered from

> BD Software, Inc.
> P.O. Box 2368
> Cambridge, MA 02238
> (617 567-3828)

Aztec C for CP/M is compatible with the Apple version. This is a good product to use when you're writing portable programs. It supports the full C-language standard. It is available from

> Manx Software Systems
> P.O. Box 55
> Shrewsbury, NJ 07701
> (201 780-4004)

Whitesmith's offers a full C compiler for the CP/M environment. You'll need a hard disk to use this product fully, however, and a large development system is recommended. Order from

> Whitesmith's, Ltd.
> 97 Lowell Road
> Concord MA 01742
> (617 369-8499)

Small C is an inexpensive, limited-feature C that is useful chiefly because the compiler is written in C and distributed in source form. This means you can modify the compiler for special applications, unusual microprocessors, etc. This was originally developed by Ron Cain in *Doctor Dobb's Journal* and is available now in many incarnations. Check your local computer bulletin board or CP/M user's group for availability.

APPLE][

Although the Apple][was among the pioneers in personal computing, it lags in C programming technology. The only C compiler available for the Apple][is Aztec C.

Aztec C is a standard version of C. It features a "shell" that brings some of the power of Unix and MS-DOS to the Apple. You can compile programs to run under the shell or to stand alone under Apple's DOS. The compiler can produce object code, "pseudo-code," which is smaller but slower, or assembler language. The package includes the compiler, an assembler, an editor, plus a linker and several additional utilities. It is available from

Manx Software Systems
P.O. Box 55
Shrewsbury, NJ 07701
(201 780-4004)

MACINTOSH

Although there are many C compilers available for the Macintosh, including Aztec C, Mac-C, and Softworks C, few take advantage of the Macintosh's many user-friendly features such as windows and pull-down menus. One exception is the Hippo-C compiler. It provides on-screen tutorials and a separate command window, and it permits simultaneous display of the old and new versions of a program.

Level 1 of Hippo-C is designed for the first-time user. It includes a full-screen editor, run-time interpreter, debugger, and a Unix-like command shell. Macintosh users will appreciate that it also provides access to the Macintosh Toolbox and Quickdraw routines. Floating-point variables are not supported.

Level 2 is more than twice the price of Level 1. Its chief advantage lies in the speed of the compiled programs, which are in native 68000 code and can be linked with assembly routines. Hippo-C is available from

Hippopotamus Software
1250 Oakmead Parkway
Sunnyvale, CA 94086
(408 738-1200)

LIBRARIES

If you use a compiled C, you most certainly will be using prewritten and tested groups of functions called *libraries*. All compiled C's have at least one library containing functions that interface with the operating system they run under. Other libraries provided with compiled C's include floating-point arithmetic and support for programs that use large amounts of memory.

It is also possible to buy fraction libraries from outside vendors. These include libraries for screen handling, file access, graphics, and windowing. If you're engaged in a large programming project, you should think seriously about getting libraries to help speed development along.

The Greenleaf Functions are an extensive library of more than two hundred MS-DOS functions available for the Lattice, Computer Innovations, and C-Ware compilers. They include video, keyboard, communications, and printer support. Some have been written in assembler for speed. They are recommended if you are going to do serious IBM-PC development work. Order from

Greenleaf Software, Inc.
2101 Hickory Drive
Carrolton, TX 75006
(214 446-8641)

C Power Packs are a set of libraries for the Lattice, Computer Innovations, and C-Ware compilers. They include floating-point routines, text windows, string handling, data base, and communications functions. They are worth looking at if you are thinking of serious product development. They are available from

Software Horizons, Inc.
165 Bedford Street
Burlington, MA 01803
(617 273-4711)

WRAPPING UP

The best choice in a C language will depend on your applications. An interpreter like Introducing C will help you learn the language and write and debug short programs. A complete but expensive compiler system like C-86 is an absolute must if you plan to develop software for commercial distribution.

Remember, the capsule reviews in this chapter are not intended to be exhaustive, just to point you toward some popular products worth investigating further. Compilers and interpreters undergo constant revision, so be sure to use our compiler checklist before you buy.

One good source of up-to-date benchmark information is the *Laboratory Computer Letter*, published by Information Research, 10367 Paw Paw Lake Dr., Mattawan, MI 49071. Cost is $124 per year.

==================================

Using Your Compiler
Appendix I

This appendix explains how to use several popular C interpreters and compilers so you can run the programs presented in this book. The compilers covered in this appendix are:

- Unix Version 7 (or Xenix) C
- Lattice C (MS-DOS)
- Computer Innovations' C-86 C (MS-DOS)
- Computer Innovations' Introducing C (MS-DOS)
- Aztec C (Apple][DOS 3.3)

This guide is necessarily brief and is intended only to get you started. You may have to refer to the manuals for your compiler and operating system for specific details about editing programs and running them. For example, when you see ⟨file name⟩ in the procedures that follow, it means you are to supply the name of the program you are currently working on; the rules for naming files depend on the individual computer system.

The C compilers described in this appendix fall into two classes: *compilers* that actually create an entire program (called an *object module*) at once, and *interpreters* that execute your program a line at a time. Interpreters are much easier to use because the job of executing a program can be completed in a single step. If you are using a compiler, the job of preparing the programs in this book has three steps:

1. First, you enter the program statements using a text editor (this may or may not already be on your system). The file you create is referred to as a *source file.*

2. Next, you compile the program. This translates it into an object module containing machine-language instructions.

3. Finally, you link the program. This "glues in" extra machine-language modules to perform floating-point arithmetic, program entry and exit, and operating system functions.

If any of these three steps don't work, check your program again. If you need to change anything, you will have to repeat steps 1, 2, and 3 again. To cut down on the number of times you have to go through this hassle, carefully check your programs before you compile them. Look especially for:

- Unmatched parentheses, double quotes, single quotes, and comment marks.

- An unmatched opening or closing brace.

- Statements that don't have a semicolon after them.

- Incorrectly spelled variable names and C keywords.

If you still can't find the problem after looking over the program, then make sure it's been copied in correctly from the listing in the book. You should also check your manuals to see that you are using the compiler and linker properly.

UNIX VERSION 7 (OR XENIX) C

To run the programs in this book using Unix or Xenix, follow this procedure:

1. Edit your program using one of several editors on the system. If you have a CRT terminal, use VI (visual editor); if you have a hardcopy terminal, you'll have to use ED or EX instead. Use any name you want for the file, followed by .C (so you know it's a C-language

program file). Enter and correct the statements that make up the programs. You'll need to refer to manuals for details on how the editors work.

```
$ vi <file name>.c
```

2. To compile and link a program, use the command CC:

```
$ cc <file name>
```

Linking occurs automatically when compilation is complete. Check with your system programmer or installation manual if the default libraries and directories used by CC are correct. See Appendix II for information about additional functions your program might need. If it does, you may need to link your program separately. The commands to do this are:

```
$ cc -c <file name>
$ ld /lib/crt0.o <file name>.o <other files ...> -lc
```

3. When step 2 is completed, you'll either have errors to correct or a program you can run. If you have errors (the C compiler will print them on your screen), you'll have to go back to step 1 and correct them. If not, the program is called A.OUT in your directory. You can run the program by typing

```
$ a.out
```

4. When you're satisfied with the program, you can rename it to a more descriptive file name by typing

```
$ mv a.out <file name>
```

LATTICE C

(For the IBM PC and PC compatibles only.) To compile and link a program using Lattice C, follow this procedure:

1. Edit the program using a text editor. MS-DOS comes with a text editor program called EDLIN. EDLIN has no advantages other than being free. If you plan to do much additional programming, get a real text editor like PC-ED or Brief.

2. To compile your program, type:

```
A>lc1 <file name>
A>lc2 <file name>
```

Notice there are two phases to compilation. If either fails, you have to go back and edit your program again to correct the errors at the line numbers indicated. See the instructions at the start of this appendix for a list of common problems to look for.

3. To link your program, type:

```
A>link cs+<file name>,<file name>,nul,lcs
```

4. And to run your program, type:

```
A><file name>
```

COMPUTER INNOVATIONS' C-86 C

To compile and link a program using Computer Innovations' C-86 C, follow this procedure:

1. Edit the program using a text editor. MS-DOS comes with a text editor program called EDLIN. EDLIN has no advantages other than being free. If you plan to do much additional programming, get a real text editor.

2. To compile your program, type:

```
A>cc1 <file name>
A>cc2 <file name>
A>cc3 <file name>
A>cc4 <file name>
```

Notice there are four phases to compilation. If any of these fail, you have to go back and edit your program again to correct the errors at the line numbers indicated. See the instructions at the start of the appendix for a list of common problems to look for. Since there are four steps involved each time, you may wish to build a "batch" file to automate this process. See the C-86 C User's Guide for a sample batch file.

3. To link your program, type:

```
A>link <file name>,<file name>,nul,c86sas
```

4. And to run your program, type:

```
A><file name>
```

COMPUTER INNOVATIONS' INTRODUCING C

To run your programs with Introducing C, use the following procedure:

1. Boot your MS-DOS computer. When start-up is complete and you see the A> prompt, enter:

   `A>cme`

2. A welcoming message will appear on the screen. When you press RETURN the screen will clear. Once you are running Introducing C, you have a workspace you can use to write your program in. As in BASIC, you can read your programs into the workspace, edit them, run them, and write them to a file when you are done. The basic commands you need to use are:

   r   Reads a file into your workspace. The entire file is read after the current line you are working on. Thus you can easily append one file to another.

   w   Writes your workspace to a file. The entire workspace is written to the file you specify.

   q   Exits Introducing C and returns to MS-DOS. You'll be asked to write your file before you can quit. If you have to quit and you don't want to save your changes, use Q instead.

   a   Lets you add lines to the workspace. The lines you type are added after the line the cursor is on. Use the up or down arrow to stop entry of lines and resume entry of commands.

   i   Lets you add lines to the workspace. The lines are added before the line the cursor is on.

   PgUp   Moves the cursor back one page in the workspace.

   PgDn   Moves the cursor forward one page in the workspace.

   →   Enters "edit mode" on the current line. Subsequent →s moves the cursor character-by-character to the right.

   ←   Moves the cursor left one character in edit mode.

   Up   Moves the cursor up one line in the workspace.

Down Moves the cursor down one line in the workspace.

F2 Runs your program. The screen will clear, and output from your program will begin on the first line.

AZTEC C

Like Unix C, Aztec C has a compiler and linker. To insulate you from Apple's DOS, Aztec C uses a program called the "shell." The shell lets you enter Unix-like commands to edit, compile, and link programs instead of BRUNning them under Applesoft. Since Apples come in a variety of flavors (][plus,][e,][c, and Macintosh), refer to the Aztec C owner's manual for information on how to start the shell and configure it for your Apple. To edit, compile, and link programs under Aztec C, use the following procedure:

1. Edit the programs using VED. Refer to the Aztec C owner's manual for information on how to use VED. End the file name with .C

   ```
   -? ved <file name>.c
   ```

2. To compile the programs, use the command:

   ```
   -? cci <file name>.c
   ```

3. To link the programs for execution under the shell, use the command:

   ```
   -? ln <file name>.o fltint.lib shint.lib
   ```

   When the programs are linked in this fashion, you just need to type the file's name to run it:

   ```
   -? <file name>
   ```

4. To link the programs for execution under Apple's DOS without the shell (called stand-alone execution), use the command:

   ```
   -? ln <file name>.o fltint.lib saint.lib
   ```

   When the programs are linked this way, you must BRUN the program from Applesoft:

   ```
   ] BRUN <file name>
   ```

You may need to modify some of the programs in this book to have them run under Aztec C on the Apple. Consult Appendix II for additional details.

Franz & Good: Writing Business Programs in C Language (Chilton)

USING YOUR COMPILER

Additional Functions and Program Changes
Appendix II

ADDITIONAL FUNCTIONS

The programs presented in this book use five functions that may not be found in all C libraries. These functions simplify many of the programs in this book. We didn't include them in the text because they were too advanced for you at the time they were needed, and you already had enough to worry about. The five functions you may need to add to your library are the two utility functions, gf() and dashes(), and the three memory functions, initmem(), insert(), and delete().

The listings for these five functions are provided below. You may want to enter gf() and dashes() together in one file, and insert(), init-mem(), and delete() in another file.

When you enter a program that uses these functions, you can either copy the file containing the functions into the file on which you are are working or compile them separately and then link them into your programs. The former method is easier initially, but the latter means less typing in the long run. If you choose to link, consult your C compiler's user's manual for specifics.

```
/* Listing A2-1. Utility Functions */

float gf()
{
        char inbuf[255];
```

```
        printf("? ");
        return atof(gets(inbuf, 255));
}


dashes(n)
int n;
{
        int i;

        for (i = 0; i < n; i = i + 1) printf("-");
}



/* Listing A2-2. Memory Functions */

char _mem[8192], *_mend, *_mlast;

initmem()
{
        _mlast = &_mem[8191];
        _mend = &_mem[0];
}

insert(s, p)
char *s;
unsigned p;
{
        int count, 1;
        char *from, *to;

        1 = strlen(s) + 1;
        if (_mend+1 < _mlast) {
                from = _mend;
                to = _mend + 1;
                count = _mend - p + 1;
                while (count) {
                        *to = *from;
                        to--; from--; count--;
                }
                strcpy(p, s);
                _mend++;
                return 1;
        }
        else return 0;
}
```

```
char *delete(p)
char *p;
{
        int count;
        char *to, *from;

        if (_mend) {
                to = p;
                from = p + strlen(p) + 1;
                count = _mend - from;
                while (count) {
                        *to = *from;
                        to++; from++; count--;
                }
                return 1;
        }
        else return 0;
}
```

ADDITIONAL PROGRAM CHANGES

Besides typing the functions shown above, small changes may be needed in the programs to get them to run on certain C compilers. The following are specific changes you may need to make.

UNIX VERSION 7 C OR XENIX C

Here are the changes you need to make if you are using a Unix or Xenix C compiler:

1. At the start of each program, prior to the *main()* function, add the statements:

   ```
   #include "stdio.h"
   #include "ctype.h"
   ```

2. If the program uses *gf()*, before *main()* add the statements:

   ```
   float gf();
   extern double atof();
   ```

3. If the program uses *pow()*, *sqrt()*, or *floor()*, before *main()* add the statement:

   ```
   extern double floor(), pow(), sqrt();
   ```

4. If the program uses the Julian date functions, before *main()* add the statement:

```
float julmdy(), mjul(), djul(), yjul();
```

5. If the program uses the memory functions, add the following statement in your *main()* function:

```
initmem();
```

6. You must include the code for the functions *gf()*, *dashes()*, *initmem()*, *insert()*, and *delete()* if these functions are used in a program.

LATTICE C

Lattice C is completely compatible with Unix version 7 C. Refer to the previous section for applicable changes.

COMPUTER INNOVATIONS' C-86 C

C-86 C is completely compatible with Unix version 7 C. No additional changes are required. Refer to the Unix section above for more information.

INTRODUCING C

The following changes are required if you are using Introducing C:

1. If the program uses the memory functions, add the following statement in your *main()* function:

```
initmem();
```

2. You must include the code for the functions *gf()*, *dashes()*, *initmem()*, *insert()*, and *delete()* if these functions are used in the program.

APPLE][AZTEC C

Aztec C is nearly compatible with Unix. There were, however, bugs in our version of the compiler (1.05C) with respect to floating-point arithmetic. You should make the following changes:

1. Change all *float* variables to *double*. *double* declares a double-precision floating-point variable. This seems to solve the problems in the calendar routines.

2. At the start of each program, prior to the *main()* function, add the statement

```
#include "stdio.h"
```

==

More About Files in C
Appendix III

This appendix discusses additional techniques for manipulating files in C. Our intent is not to provide a detailed tutorial but merely to show you a few ways in which, with further study, you can increase the efficiency of your programs. One possible limitation is that these techniques, convenient and powerful as they are, are not supported by every C compiler.

ADDITIONAL ACCESS MODES

In Chapter 4, you learned that file input and output in C are done with four basic functions. The first of these functions, *fopen()*, creates a file for use in input or output. Before you can read or write to a file, it must be "opened" so that your computer's operating system can identify the file's name and allocate memory for reading or writing data. You learned in the checkbook program that *fopen()* has two arguments, the name of the file and the type of access you want, either "r" for read or "w" for write. There are, however, additional access types that you can use for more advanced file processing. Some of these are:

rb   to read the file as binary data

wb   to write the file as binary data

a   to write the file and append data to it

If the "a" access type is employed, new data will be positioned at the end of an already existing file. Without this option, fopen() will overlay an existing file, erasing its contents and replacing it with a new but empty file. By using the "a" access mode, you can provide for continuous updating of an existing file.

You will probably find less frequent use for the "rb" and "wb" access modes, which treat your file as a string of bytes rather than characters. One practical application is in building printer drivers that send special control sequences to printers or terminals. *Warning:* With the "rb" and "wb" access modes, compound characters like a return followed by a linefeed will not be turned into the single character \n, and on some systems the end-of-file character control-Z will not be processed. Consult your C-language manuals for more specific information.

ADDITIONAL FUNCTIONS

For the majority of programs that you write, you can get by with the four basic file-handling functions *fopen()*, *fclose()*, *fgets()*, and *fprintf()*. If you are writing more complicated programs, however, you may need more advanced functions, such as:

fgetc(file)
> Gets a single character from *file* and returns it or, if the file is at its end, the value −1. Here *file* is not the name of a file but its file descriptor, the number that was returned when you opened it. You would want to process single characters in a file if you were writing text-processing programs or programs that directly control devices such as terminals and printers.

fputc(char, file)
> Puts the single character *char* to the file *file*. If the file has been opened with "w," a \n character will be processed correctly. If the file has been opened with "wb," you'll get just a linefeed character instead. This function returns a −1 if an error occurs (e.g., the diskette is full, the drive door is not closed); otherwise, it returns zero. Like the function *fgetc()* shown above, fputc() is used in programs that directly control terminals and printers or perform character-by-character processing of a file.

fputs(s, file)
> Puts the string *s* to the file *file*. Characters are sent to the file until a null byte (the end of the string) is detected. A −1 is returned if an

error occurs (e.g., the diskette is full, the file is not open); otherwise, a zero is returned. *fputs()* will speed up your programs since, unlike *fprintf()*, it doesn't do any formatting.

fflush(file)

Writes all buffered data and control information to the file on disk. While you are writing to your files, not all data is actually on the disk. Instead, it is "buffered," held in memory until a later time. If your program or computer were to crash before the data was actually written, you could lose this information. You can use this function at key points in your program to save important data in case of a crash.

sprintf(s, format, arg1, . . .)

This function is a cousin of *fprintf()*. Instead of requiring a file to write the output to, however, it uses a string *s* instead. This means you can build strings in memory by using the same formatting characters you use with *printf()* and *fprintf()*. Why do this? One of the most common uses of *sprintf()* is to build format strings for *fprintf()*. You can easily control field formats and lengths by building the appropriate format string with *sprintf()*, then go ahead and print the output in the format you created using *fprintf()*.

stdin, *stdout*, AND *stderr*

When you run your C programs, three files are always automatically opened for your use. These are called *stdin* (standard input), *stdout* (standard output), and *stderr* (standard error). The first two, *stdin* and *stdout*, usually point to the terminal from which you're running the program. In fact, when you use the functions *gets()* and *printf()*, it is exactly as if you had used *fgets()* with *stdin* and *fprintf()* with *stdout*. Since getting input from and displaying messages to the terminal are so commonplace, these shorthand functions are available and are more widely used.

The third file, *stderr*, always points to the terminal. You use it for printing error and warning messages you don't want added to *stdout*, which is usually reserved for the "legitimate" output of the program.

REDIRECTING I/O

If you write your programs to process *stdin* and *stdout* instead of your own files, you can take advantage of a C feature called *redirected I/O*. This means you can tell your C program to read standard input and write standard output to and from files on disk or a printer rather than to and from the terminal. With most computer operating systems, you redirect input from the terminal to another file by placing a less-than symbol (<) in front of a file name on the program's command line. Similarly, you redirect output from the video display to a disk file by placing a greater-than symbol (>) in front of a file name.

For example, if you named the statistics program developed in Chapter 5 "STATS," you could send the report you saw at your terminal to a file called REPORT by typing

```
stats >report
```

when you ran the program. You can even send the report directly to the system printer with a command line such as

```
stats >/dev/lpt
```

if you are running your program on a Unix or Xenix system, or

```
stats >lpt1:
```

if you are using an IBM PC C compiler.

Take advantage of redirecting I/O to make your own programs more general and flexible. For example, suppose you use the popular word processing program WordStar in an IBM PC under MS-DOS and want to look at some files you created with it. Normally, WordStar places extra bits of information in files, which are unreadable if you try to display them with commands such as TYPE. The following program, when compiled and linked properly, can be used to convert WordStar files into "normal" text files that you can look at directly:

```
/* Convert WordStar Files to Readable Text */

main()
{
        char c;

        while ((c = fgetc(stdin)) != -1)
                fputc(c & 0x7f, stdout);
        exit();
}
```

If this looks simple, it's because it is simple. By using the files *stdin* and *stdout*, we've let C handle the chore of opening and closing the files for us.

If we call this program "WSTOASC" (short for "WordStar to ASCII") we can convert a WordStar file such as MYFILE.WS to MYFILE.TXT (a plain ASCII version) with the command:

```
wstoasc <myfile.ws >myfile.asc
```

and then look at our file with the MS-DOS command TYPE:

```
type myfile.asc
```

Notice also in this program that we used two of the functions discussed earlier in this appendix, *fgetc()* and *fputc()*, to process individual characters in the file. In particular, the statement

```
fputc(c & 0x7f, stdout);
```

copies the character read from the file *stdin* to *stdout* and removes the eighth bit from it in the process. (The ampersand (&) used in this manner means "logical AND.") Just be sure you type in the spaces in this statement *exactly* as shown if you decide to enter and run this procedure. Using *fgetc()* and *fputc()* also means that we don't have to declare character arrays to hold strings during processing and we don't have to write a loop with a *for* statement to process each character in the array. This keeps the program nice and simple.

A WORD ABOUT PORTABILITY

Unfortunately, some of the C functions shown in this appendix may function differently with certain brands of compilers or interpreters. To be on the safe side, check each function in your user's manual before you try to use it in your own programs. In particular, command line arguments and device names vary greatly from system to system. To help you get started, a summary of the changes needed when working with any of the four most popular C compilers is provided in Appendix II of this book.

Franz & Good: Writing Business Programs in C Language (Chilton)

MORE ABOUT FILES IN C

Statistical Functions
Appendix IV

In Chapter 5, you wrote a program that processed files created by your electronic checkbook and computed basic statistics, including the number of items in the checkbook, their total, their mean, and their standard deviation. In this appendix you develop additional, more advanced statistical functions in C for use with this program or with other programs that you write. These functions have been included for the benefit of engineers, scientists, and others who are familiar with similar programs written in other computer languages. Included here are functions for computing covariances and correlations, fitting least-squares regression lines, and computing ranks (a prerequisite to almost all nonparametric statistical procedures).

MEAN AND VARIANCE REVISITED

Although it may seem that we have already written a procedure to compute mean and variance in Chapter 5, that procedure had a potentially fatal flaw. Recall that in that procedure we maintained two running totals, one of the observations and one of their squares:

```
total = total + data;
sumsq = sumsq + pow(data, 2.0);
```

Once all the data had been read in, we used these totals to compute the standard deviation:

```
stddev = sqrt((sumsq - total*total/n)/(n-1));
```

But what if the totals are large while their difference is quite small? (An example would be the totals 1,000,000 and 1,000,002.) Then, because a *float* number can hold only a certain number of digits, we may lose track of the difference. To minimize the possibility of rounding errors, we'll rewrite the procedure as shown in the following listing so that the variance is computed in two stages: First we sum the observations and compute their mean, then we sum the squares of the deviations from the mean.

LISTING

```
stats(fd)
unsigned fd;
{
        int n, i;
        char rec[80];
        float data, temp[1000], total, average, sumsq, stddev;

        /* initialize variables */
        n = 0;
        total = 0;
        average = 0;
        sumsq = 0;

        /* get data from file and compute average */
        printf("\nReading");
        while (fgets(rec, 80, fd) != 0) {
                sscanf(rec, "%d %f", &i, &data);
                total = total + data;
                temp[n++] = data;
                printf(".");
        }
        printf("\n");
        average = total/n;
```

```
/* sum squares of deviates and print results */
for (k=0; k<n; ++k){
        sumsq = sumsq + (temp[k]-average)*(temp[k]-average);
        }
stddev = sqrt(sumsq/(n-1));
printf("There were %d records read\n\n", n);
printf("The total is.............. %10.2f\n", total);
printf("The standard deviation is %10.2f\n", stddev);
}
```

SAMPLE RUN

We can't show you a sample run, since we wrote this routine deliberately as a function that must be called from a *main()* program. If you want to test the procedure, you can use the *main()* you developed in Chapter 5. The results should be identical; now you can place complete confidence in the accuracy of the results even when very large numbers are involved.

NOTES

When we use the array *temp* to hold our intermediate calculations we lose some of the generality of our previous efforts. We are forced to declare *temp* as having some fixed number of data points. We could have declared *temp* [100] or *temp*[3], but this would have limited us to data sets with 100 or 3 points at most. To be on the safe side, we "guessed" there would be never more than 1,000 data points and declared *temp* [1000]. Why didn't we choose *temp*[100000]? Simple: When we declare an array we are actually setting aside space in memory; there simply isn't room for 100,000 data points in our computer. Hence the compromise. (There is a way to allocate memory for the array "as needed," but this technique is beyond the scope of this book.) The beauty of our original procedure (Chapter 5) is that we didn't have to make any guesstimates about how many data points to save.

We used two similar-looking expressions in the listing above—n++ and ++k. Although they look similar, they have quite different effects. The statement

```
temp[n++] = data;
```

stores data in *temp[n]* and then increments *n* by 1. Had we written

```
temp [++n] = data;
```

n would have been incremented *before* the data was stored. Suppose *n* is 0 to begin with. Then the statement

```
temp[n++] = data
```

leaves data stored in *temp[0]* while

```
temp[++n] = data;
```

leaves data stored in *temp[1]*. In either case, *n* would have the value 1 after the statement is executed.

COVARIANCE AND CORRELATION

With very little extra effort, we can expand the previous procedure to provide for reading in two (or more) covariates and then compute the covariances and correlations. Three covariates are used in the listing below so you may gain familiarity with some of the procedures needed to handle larger numbers of variables.

LISTING

```
stats(fd)
unsigned fd;
{
    int n, i;
    char rec[80];
    float depend, ind1, ind2, buf[3], temp [1000], avg[3], cov[9]
        corr[9];

    /* initialize variables */
    n = 0;
    avg[1]=avg[2]=avg[3]=0;
    for (i=0; i<9; ++i) {cov[i]=corr[i]=0};
```

```
/* get data from file and compute averages */
printf("\nReading");
while (fgets(rec, 80, fd) != 0) {
    sscanf(rec, "%d %f", &i, &depend, &ind1, &ind2);
    buf[1] = depend; buf [2] = ind1; buf[3] = ind2;
    for (k=0; k<3; ++k){
            avg[k] = avg [k] + buf[k];
            temp[k*100 + n] = buf[k];
            }
    n++;
    printf(".");
    }
printf("\n");
for (k=0; k<3; ++k){
    avg[k] = avg[k]/n;
    }

/* compute covariances and correlations */
for (j=0; j<n; ++j){
    for (k1=0; k1<3; ++k1){
        j1 = k1*100 + k;
        for (k2=k1; k2<3; ++2){
            k = [3*k1 + k2]
            j2 = k2*100 + k;
            cov[k] = cov[k] + (temp[j1]-avg[k1])*
                    (temp[j2]-avg[k2]);
            }
        }
    }

/* print the results */
printf("There were %d records read\n\n", n);
printf("The means are ..........");
for (k1=0; k1<3; ++k1){
    printf(%10.2f, avg[k1]);
    }
printf("The correlations are\n");
for (k1=0; k1<3; ++k1){
    printf(\n);
    for (k2=k1; k2<3; ++k2){
        k = [3*k1 + k2]
        corr[k] = cov[k]/sqrt(cov[k1]*cov[k2]);
        printf(%d10.2f, corr[k]);
        }
    }
}
```

Franz & Good: Writing Business Programs in C Language (Chilton)

STATISTICAL FUNCTIONS

NOTES

In order that this procedure be easily generalized to any number of covariates, the variables *avg*, *cov*, and *corr* were defined as arrays rather than single variables. We used nested *for* loops to ensure that we would run through all possible combinations of the variables taken two at a time. The printed result is a triangular matrix with 1s along the diagonal. Why a triangle? Because covariance and correlation are symmetric and the entries below the diagonal are identical to those above.

We used the minimum of print statements in our routine. It is up to you to format the results using the techniques you learned in the final chapters of the book.

MULTILINEAR REGRESSION

To find the coefficients b[0], b[1], and b[2] that minimize the sum of squares about the regression line

```
depend = b[0] + b[1]*ind1 + b[2]*ind2
```

we merely need to add the following statements to the preceding listing:

```
b[1] = cov[1]/cov[4];
b[2] = cov[2]/cov[8];
b[0] = avg[0] — b[1]*avg[1] - b[2]*avg[2]
```

Since we want to generalize our procedures for any number of covariates, let's rewrite these statements in a *for* loop:

```
b[0] = avg [0];
for (k=0; k<3; ++k){
     b[i] = cov[i]/cov[4*i];
     b[0] = b[0] - b[i]*avg[i];
}
```

(Whoops, don't forget to declare the array b[3] at the beginning of the listing.)

RANK TESTS

Many nonparametric statistical tests like the Wilcoxon Rank test and the Kruskal-Wallace are derived from the corresponding parametric tests. The nonparametric equivalent is obtained by replacing the numeric value of each observation with its rank in the combined sample. This conversion from the raw observation to the corresponding rank minimizes the impact of extreme observations or outliers and other similar deviations from normality.

The simplest way to obtain a set of ranks is to sort the observations and then replace each observation by its position in the sort. You could easily use the sort routine described on page 108 for this purpose. The problem with a standard sort routine is that you still need a way to keep track of the sample or treatment group from which each ranked observation was derived. The procedure below does this efficiently. It gains this efficiency by calculating and saving only the sums of the ranks of the observations in each group and not the individual ranks. For your convenience, we've added an input routine so you can immediately use the procedure to test your data.

DESCRIPTION

The data is read into a temporary array (called *data*) sample-by-sample so that the observations of one sample precede those of the next. The largest element of the array is located and its rank added to the cumulative rank of the corresponding sample. Then that element is zeroed (actually it is set equal to −32,000) and the next largest element is located. The function terminates after all elements have been zeroed and the values in the rank vector are used to compute the test statistic. (Note that the individual ranks are discarded and only the sum of the ranks for each sample is maintained.) If there are two samples, the Wilcoxon Rank-Sum statistic is employed. If there are more than two samples, the Kruskal-Wallace One-Way ANOVA statistic is used.

LISTING

```
main()
{
    int i, fl, j, k, m, n, nsamp, ncumobs[10], nobs[10], ntot,
        samp, obs;
    float data[300], rank[10], test, temp, denom, num, big;

    printf("How many samples are there?");
    nsamp = gn();
    printf("Enter the data from the first sample.\n");
    i = 0;
    for (j=0; j<nsamp; j++){
        printf("Press return after each observation.\n");
        printf("Enter 32000 when through entering data for this
            sample.\n");
        ncumobs[j]=i; fl = gn();
        while (fl != 32000){
                data[i++] = fl;
                fl = gn();
                }
        nobs[j]= i - ncumobs[j];
        if (j != nsamp-1) printf("Enter the data from the next
            sample.\n");
        }
    ntot = ncumobs[nsamp] = i;
    printf("Please wait one moment. I'm computing the rank sums.");
    for (k = 0; k < ntot; ++k){
        big = -32000;
         for (j = 0; j < nsamp; ++j){
            for (m = ncumobs[j]; m < ncumobs[j+1]; ++m){
                if (big < data [m]){
                        big = data [m]; samp = j; obs= m;
                        }
                }
        printf(".");
        }
    data [obs] = -32000;
    rank [samp] = rank [samp] + ntot - k;
    }
```

```
if (nsamp=2){
    /* Wilcoxon Rank-Sum Test */
    temp  = (ntot + 1)/2;
    num   = nobs[0]*temp;
    denom = nobs[0]*nobs[1]*temp/6;
    test  = (rank [0] - num)/sqrt(denom);
    printf ("\nThe Rank Sum test took the value%10.2f.", test);
    }


if (nsamp > 2){
    /* Kruskal-Wallace One-Way ANOVA */
    test = 0;
    for (i=0; i < nsamp; i++){
        test = test + rank[i]*rank[i]/nobs[i];
        }
    test = (12*test/ntot/(ntot+1)) - 3*(ntot +1);
    printf ("Kruskal-Wallace took the value,%10.2f.", test);
    }
}
```

SAMPLE RUN

How many samples are there?

2

Enter the data from the first sample.
Press return after each observation.
Enter 32000 when through entering data for this sample.

12
15
11
19
32000

Enter the data from the next sample.
Press return after each observation.
Enter 32000 when through entering data for this sample.

14
25
27
32000

Franz & Good: Writing Business Programs in C Language (Chilton)

STATISTICAL FUNCTIONS

175

```
Please wait one moment. I'm computing the rank sums...............

The Rank Sum test took the value -1.41.
```

NOTES

Again, here is a procedure that is easily modified to fit your specific statistical needs. For example, it could be modified to accept floating-point data. Or you could extend it to provide for a two-way analysis of variance using ranks. You will also want to strengthen the procedure to make it completely error-proof: What if $nsamp = 1$? (a mistake, but mistakes will happen). What if the user fails to enter any data in one of the treatment groups? What if there are ties among the observations?

==

C Program
Refresher
Appendix V

Here's a summary of the C programming language as presented in this book. Use it as a checklist when you write your programs.

BEFORE YOU START

Before you write your program, you should have at least:

1. A brief, specific, English-language description of what you want the program to do. It should be about a paragraph in length and describe what the completed program is intended to accomplish.

2. An English-language "design" of the main function and major sub-functions of the program. This design should tell how the program is going to accomplish the goal described in step 1. Look at the design of the checkbook or statistics programs for examples.

THE *main()* FUNCTION

The *main()* function for your program is organized like this:

```
/* Comment telling what the program does, when it was last changed,
   and by whom
*/
```

```
#include files needed (see Appendix II)
global variables needed by all functions;

main()
{
    local variables used by main();

    statements that make up main();
}
```

Not all programs need global variables; use as few global variables as possible since they can make your program hard to maintain.

DECLARING VARIABLES

To declare variables, start by specifying the type. The valid types are:

int	integer
unsigned	unsigned integer (address)
char	character
float	floating-point

Then specify a list of variables with that type. Specify whether each variable in the list is a simple variable, a pointer, or an array. Simple variables consist of a name only, pointers have an asterisk in front of them, and arrays are followed by the size enclosed in brackets. Refer to Chapters 2, 3, and 4 for more information in declaring and using variables.

USING FUNCTIONS

To organize your program, reduce conflicts in naming, simplify debugging, and speed program modification, lay out your program as a series of functions instead of just writing statement after statement. To call a function, use its name and (optional) pass it arguments:

```
name(arg1, arg2, ...)
```

The function must be defined somewhere else in your program or library. Use this template to define a function:

/* Comment telling what the function does */

```
name(arg1, arg2, ...)
declarations of arg1, arg2, ...;
{
        declarations of variables local to function;

        statements that make up the function;

}
```

The declarations in your subfunctions work exactly like they do in the *main()* function. The number and type of arguments declared in the function header must exactly match the number and type of arguments you pass to the function. You use a *return* statement to pass a value back to the caller. Refer to Chapter 2 for more information about how to define and use functions.

USING STATEMENTS

The statements you'll be using in your functions are:

variable = expression;
This is a simple assignment statement that takes the result of the expression and puts it in the variable.

if (expression) statement;
The expression is evaluated. If it is nonzero, it is considered true and the statement is executed. If not, it is skipped.

else statement;
If the expression in a matching *if* statement was zero (false), this statement is executed. If it was true, then this statement is skipped. The *else* statement must always be paired with an *if* statement or an error results.

while (expression) statement 1;
While the expression is true, statement 1 is repeatedly executed. Something in statement 1 had better change something in the expression or the program will loop forever.

for (expression 1; expression 2; expression 3) statement 1;
This statement creates a loop with expression 1 performing setup,

expression 2 testing if the loop continues, and expression 3 executing at the end of every pass through the loop. If the loop is to end, something in expression 3 must change something that will make expression 2 false. While the loop runs, statement 1 is executed.

break;

Immediately transfers control out of a *while* or *for* loop to the first statement following the loop. This statement gives you a way to break out of a loop if an error occurs. You also use *break* to end an individual *case* in a *switch* statement.

switch (expression) statement 1;

This statement is used to compare the expression against multiple "cases" (shown below). Statement 1 here is really a series of *case* and *default* statements, one of which will be executed.

case (constant expression): statement;

Describes an individual case in a switch-case statement. The switch expression is compared with the constant expression. If true (that is, the constant and the expression are equal), the statement is executed. Otherwise, control resumes at the next case or default statement.

default: statement;

If none of the individual *case* statements in a *switch* was executed, then this statement will be executed. This statement is always the last one in a *switch.*

return (expression);

This statement is used to return a value to the caller of a function. The result of (expression) is substituted for the name of the function back in the calling statement.

{ statement 1; statement 2; . . .}

You can enclose a series of several statements with {} to have them treated as if they were a single statement. This method is used in *if, else, while, for,* and *switch* statements.

More information on individual C statements can be found in Chapters 2 and 3.

USING EXPRESSIONS

Wherever (expression) appears in the preceding statements, you can write expressions involving constants, variables, and function calls. You can use parentheses to organize hard-to-read expressions, and you can use these operators in your expressions:

+	addition
−	subtraction
*	multiplication
/	division
%	remainder
++	increment (adds 1)
−−	decrement (subtracts 1)
−	negation (if used by itself)
‖	logical OR (one or other must be nonzero)
&&	logical AND (both must be nonzero)
<	less than
>	greater than
>=	greater than or equal to
<=	less than or equal to
==	equals
!=	not equals

In statements that perform looping and branching, such as *if*, an expression is considered true if it evaluates to a nonzero quantity and false if it evaluates to zero.

USING CONSTANTS

Constants in C statements are one of the following items:

a sequence of digits with or without a sign (integer)

an integer with a decimal point and/or exponent (float)

a single character enclosed in single quotes (character)

a sequence of characters enclosed in quotes (string)

Some "magic" character constants are:

\n   return and linefeed (newline)

\t   tab character

\f   formfeed character

\b   backspace character

\\   single backslash

\"   quotation mark

SOME IMPORTANT FUNCTIONS

Here are some essential C functions presented throughout the book:

atof()	converts string to floating-point
atoi()	converts string to integer
exit()	exits program and returns to system
fclose()	closes a file when done processing
fgets()	reads a string from file
floor()	rounds floating-point number down
fopen()	opens a file for processing
fprintf()	sends format output to file
gets()	reads a string from terminal
islower()	returns "true" if lowercase character
isupper()	returns "true" if uppercase character
pow()	exponent function
printf()	sends formatted output to terminal
strcmp()	returns 0 if strings are equal
strcpy()	copies one string to another
strlen()	returns length of string in characters
tolower()	converts character to lowercase
toupper()	converts character to uppercase

Franz & Good: Writing Business Programs in C Language (Chilton)

C PROGRAM REFRESHER

SUBSCRIPTS AND POINTERS

Generally, whenever you use an array you have the option of using either subscripts or pointer variables to access it. Choose the method that makes the function more readable.

Subscripts in C begin at zero and run to *one less* than the number of items specified when the array was declared. For example, to process

```
char array[10];
```

your *for* statement would be:

```
for (i = 0; i < 10; i++) ...
```

Whenever you work with strings, remember to add an additional character in your arrays for the null character at the end of the string.

Remember that addition and subtraction move a pointer to the next or previous item of the same size, not to the address one byte higher or lower. In other words, don't add 4 to a *float* pointer if you want to point at the next floating-point number—add 1.

COMMON BUG LIST

If your program doesn't compile or run, the reason may be that:

1. You are missing a semicolon (;) on the statement before the one that seems to be in error.

2. You've misspelled a variable name or statement keyword.

3. Your () and {} don't match.

4. You haven't declared a variable or function properly.

5. The number or type of arguments passed to a function doesn't match what is declared in the function's header.

6. You haven't declared a function's type (you have to do this if the function returns anything other than an *int*).

7. You are exceeding the dimensions of an array with a loop or pointer expression. Unlike BASIC or FORTRAN, C won't let you know when this happens.

Once again, good luck in developing your own C programs. We hope C will increase your productivity, too.

Franz & Good: Writing Business Programs in C Language (Chilton)

Index

access types, for file processing, 162–163
add() function, for checkbook program,
    71–72
address operator (&), 100, 102
addresses
    calculations with, 100
    passing with pointers, 101
    variable containing, 99
again() function, in statistics program,
    90, 95
amortization schedule program, 18–22
annuity, 11
Apple
    C compiler for, 148–149
    linking and compiling C programs on,
    156
arguments, 179
    declaration statements for, 24
    passed to function, 25
arithmetic in C, 12
array element, 49
    pointer to represent, 138
arrays, 49, 172
    access with subscripts or pointers,
    182
    address of last character in, 65
    allocation of memory for, 169

comparison of, 103
    declaration of, 166, 178
ASCII code, 47
    converting WordStar files to, 165–166
ask() function, 75, 77
assembler interface, to library, 144
assignment statement, 179
atof() function, 80
atoi() function, 78, 79
Aztec C (Manx Software Systems), 121,
    148–149
    linking and compiling process for, 156
    program changes required by, 160–161

BDS C (BD Software), 147–148
backslash, 48, 128
    character constants with, 182
    and *printf()* function, 55
backspace character (\b), 48
benchmark problem, 17
braces, 6–7
    to designate compound statement, 28
    and *for* statement, 20
brackets
    for arrays, 49
    empty, 54
break statement, 39, 180

bubble sort, 110
buffered data, 164
bugs, eliminating. *See* debugging process

C-86 compiler, 141–142, 150
C Food Smorgasbord, 146
CP/M-based computers
    C compiler available for, 147–148
    C interpreter for, 142
C Power Packs, 150
C programming language, 1–2
C Programming Language (Kernighan
    and Ritchie), 138, 143, 146
C-Ware C, 147
    library for, 150
Cain, Ron, 148
calendar, perpetual. *See* perpetual
    calendar program
calling function, 24, 27, 34
    nested, 31
case statement, 180. *See also switch-
    case* statement
center() function, 56–57, 58
character arrays, 46, 49
character string, 50
character variables, 46–49
    declaring, 48
characters
    compound, 163
    converting to uppercase, 66, 95
    getting from file, 163
    putting in file, 163
checkbook program
    changing data contents, 78, 81–82
    main() function for, 65–70
    printing register, 128–131, 131–135
    restrictions of, 114
    uses for, 116
comments, in C, 5, 94, 126, 177
compilers, 140, 142–143
    and function portability, 166
    selection features, 143–146
    using, 151–156
compound characters, 163
compound statements, 28, 180
Computer Innovations' C-86 C, 121, 146–
    147
    compiling and linking process for,
    154
    library for, 150
    program changes required by, 160

Computer Innovations' Introducing C,
    141–142, 150
    process for running programs with,
    155–156
constants, 181–182
    expressed as variables, 125
control-Z, 163
conversions of type, with *sscanf()*
    function, 77
correlation, 170–172
covariance, 170–172
crash, and loss of buffered data, 164

dashes() function, 10, 14, 158, 160
data
    buffered, 164
    initializing, 93
    preventing accidental destruction of, 91
data file, 118
dates
    calculation of interval between, 33–34
    conversion program, 27–30
    program for week-day determination,
    35–38
debugging process, 13, 152, 183
    with compiler, 143
    and interpreters, 141
declaration, 7–8, 53–54, 179
    of character arrays, 166
    of character variable, 48
    of external variables and arguments,
    24
    of function type, 26
    of global variables, 108–109
    of pointers, 99
    of string size, 51
    of variables, 67, 178
decrement operator (− −), 105
default statement, 180
#define, 139–140
delete() function, 110, 159, 160
    for checkbook, 74–78
detail, 118
detail() function, 122, 124, 126, 136
    modifying, 128
diff() function, 132, 135
djul() function, 27, 30
Doctor Dobb's Journal, 148
documentation, with compiler, 145
double, 161
dow() function, 40, 41

EDLIN, 153
8-bit CP/M-based computer, C interpreter for, 142
else statement, 28, 30, 179
end-of-file character, 163
endless loop, 42–43
English-language description, as design technique, 64, 177
erasing files, 83
error checking, for file name, 89
escape character, 48
escape character constants, 182
exec() function, 144
execution speed. *See* speed of execution
exit() function, 66
expressions, 180–181
   arithmetic, 12
Extended Binary Coded Decimal Interchange Code (EBCDIC), 47
external variables, declaration statements for, 24

fclose() function, 83
fflush() function, 164
fgetc() function, 163, 166
fgets() function, 82–83, 164
file descriptor, 84, 91, 92
   for printer, 122
   returned by *fopen()*, 82
file name
   error checking, 89
   getting from user, 91–92
   for printer, 121
files
   adding to, 163
   naming, 83
   opening, 162–163
   reading and writing, 82–83
   redirection to, 164–166
   treatment of printer as, 121
fill() function, 55–56, 58
find() function, 75–78
float, 131–132
floating-point numbers, 8, 9, 143
   converting string to, 80
floor() function, 30, 159
fopen() function, 82, 84, 91, 92, 144, 162–163
for loops, 41
   nested, 172

for statement, 18–20, 179–180
   compared to *while* statement, 38
   compound statement with, 28
   relational operators in, 29
format
   of data records, 88
   in *printf()* function, 8, 52
   of program listings, 32
formatting reports, 117–120
formfeed (\f), 48
fprintf() function, 82–83, 126, 136, 164
fputc() function, 163, 166
fputs() function, 163–164
fread() function, 144
function definition, 24
functions, 2–3, 23–27, 178–179, 182
   arguments in (*See* arguments)
   calling, 24, 27, 34
   declaration of type, 26
   defined, 6
   libraries of, 149–150
   listings. *See* listings
   nested call, 31
   and pointers, 101
   return value of, 41, 180
   variables declared within, 67

getfile() function, 91–92, 97, 122
   in statistics program, 90
gets() function, 51, 55, 75, 126, 164
gf() function, 8, 14, 157–158, 159, 160
global variables, 66, 122, 132, 178
   declaration, 108–109
   for lines and pages of reports, 122
Greenleaf Functions, 150

header, 24
headings, 118
Hippo-C compiler (Hippopotamus Software), 149

if statement, 179
   compound statement with, 28
   relational operators in, 29
if-else statements, 28, 30
   nesting, 34
#*include*, 139, 178
increment operator (++), 41, 109, 169–170
indentations, in program listings, 32

initializing data, 93
initmem() function, 158, 160
input/output, redirected, 164–166
insert() function, 71, 110, 158, 160
Instant C (Rational Systems, Inc.), 142
integers, 36
    converting string to, 79
    variable as, 35
interpreters, 140–142, 151–152
    and function portability, 166
Introducing C (Computer Innovations,
    Inc.), 141–142, 150, 155–156

Julian date, defined, 27
Julian date functions, 160
Julian format
    conversion to date, 30–31
    date conversion program, 27–30
julmdy() function, 27, 132

Kaypro, C interpreter for, 142
Kernighan, Bryan W., 138
Kruskal-Wallace test, 173, 174

label() function, 53, 54, 124, 126
Laboratory Computer Letter, 150
Lattice C, 146
    compiling and linking process for, 153–
    154
    library for, 150
    program changes required by, 159–160
lease/purchase decision program, 6–11
left-corner construction, as design
    technique, 65
libraries, 144, 149–150
Lifeboat Associates, 146
lines, number per page, 119
linker, 145
linking, 142
list() function, for checkbook, 72–73
listings
    add() function for checkbook, 71
    again() function, 95
    amortization schedule program, 20–21
    ask() function for checkbook, 77
    centering strings function, 57
    check register program, 129–131, 132–
    135
    checkbook change component, 81
    checkbook *main()* function, 69–70

conversion from Julian format to date,
    30–31
dashes() function, 158
date conversion program, 27–28
date interval calculation program, 33–
    34
delete() function, 159
detail() function, 126–127, 130–131, 134
diff() function, 135
dow() function, 40
fill string with character function, 56
find() function for checkbook, 78
generic report program, 123–124
getfile() function, 92
gf() function, 157–158
initmem() function, 158
insert() function, 158
Julian date functions testing, 32
label() function, 54, 126
lease/purchase decision program, 7,
    10–11
list() function for checkbook, 73
load() function for checkbook, 84–85
mail label program, 54, 126–127
mdys() function, 135
memory functions, 158–159
mortgage payment program, 14–15
newline() function, 124
newpage() function, 124, 130, 133
openprt() function, 123
order() function, 111
perpetual calendar program, 39–40,
    43–44, 58–60
present value calculation program, 16–
    17
rank test, 174–175
readin() function, 111
save() function for checkbook, 85
select() function, 104, 106
sorting functions, 111–112
statistics program *main()* function, 91
stats() function, 94, 168–169, 170–172
strncpy() function for checkbook, 107
summary() function, 127, 134
title() function for calendar, 59–60
utility functions, 157–158
week-day determination for date
    program, 37–38
WordStar file conversion, 165–166
writeout() function, 111

load() function, 84–85, 93, 97
local variables, 66, 178
loops, 179–180. *See also for* loops
    endless, 42–43
    exit from, 72
    while, 42, 66, 90
lseek() function, 144

MS-DOS operating system, C compiler for
    use with, 146–147
Macintosh, C compilers for, 149
magic numbers, 125, 140
mailing labels program, 53–55
    printing routine, 124–128
main() function, 177–178
    for checkbook program, 65–70
    for generic report program, 118, 121–
      124
    for lease program, 6–7
    for mailing labels program, 53
    for statistics program, 89–91
    in test program, 32
    Manz Software Systems (Aztec C), 148,
      149
mdys() function, 132, 135
mean, 167–169
memory functions, 158–159
_mend, 65–66, 71, 72, 100
Microsoft, 146
mjul() function, 27, 31
mortgage payment program, 11–15
multilinear regression, 172

nested *for* loops, 172
nested function call, 31
nested *while* statements, 105
newline (\n), 10, 48, 53, 84
newline() function, 122, 124
newpage() function, 122, 124, 130, 133
nonparametric statistical tests, 173–176
null character (\0), 48, 50, 84
numbers
    floating-point, 8, 9, 80, 143
    unsigned, 68

object module, 142, 151, 152
openprt() function, 122, 123
operators
    arithmetic, 12
    in expressions, 181
    relational, 29

order() function, 111
overlays, 145

page break, 118
pages, counting during print process, 119
payback period, program to calculate, 6–
    11
performance, as feature of C compiler,
    144–145
perpetual calendar program, 23, 38–45
    modified, 42–45, 58–60
pointer expressions, 100
pointers, 99–101, 137–138, 182
    declaration of, 178
    incrementing value of, 99
    to structures, 138
portability
    as feature of C compiler, 143–144
    of functions, 166
pow() function, 14, 159
preprocessor, 139
present value, program to calculate, 15–
    17
printer, 120–121
printer file, 118
printf() function, 8, 10, 22, 52, 126, 164
    calculations within, 11
    in mailing labels program, 53
printing, form alignment before, 128
program listings, *See* listings
programming techniques, 63–65, 74, 82.
    See also software design

qsort() function, 110
Quay, C interpreter for, 142
quicksort, 110
quotation marks, for enclosing string, 50

rank tests, 173–176
Rational Systems, Inc. (Instant C), 142
read() function, 144
readin() function, in sort process, 108,
    109, 111
reading from files, 82–83
redirected I/O, 164–166
relational operators, 29
repetition of program, 42–43
reports
    designing, 136
    formatting program for, 117–120
    generic, functions for, 121–124

return statement, 41, 179, 180
Ritchie, Dennis M., 138
Rolodex file, electronic, 113–116

save() function, 84, 85
saving data, 164
scaffold, 32, 65
scope, of variable, 66, 67
select() function, 103–108
semicolons, and *for* statement, 20
shell, 156
Small C, 148
software design, 82, 97. *See also*
    programming techniques
  flexibility, 165–166
  planning, 177
Software Horizons, Inc., 150
sort() function, 108, 110, 112
sorting, 108–113, 173
  and pointers, 138
source file, 152
  and *#include*, 139
source-level debugger, 143
source librarian program, 145
source program, 142
specifications, for program components,
    74
speed of execution
  and *fputs()* function, 164
  of search function, 107–108
  of sort process, 113
sprintf() function, 164
sqrt() function, 159
sscanf() function, 75–77, 88, 128, 129,
    136
  and pointers, 101
statements, 179–180
  compound, 28, 180
statistical functions, 167–176
statistics program
  main() function for, 89–91
  planning, 87–90
statistics, processing, 93–94
stats() function, 90, 93–94, 168–169,
    170–172
stderr, 164
stdin file, 164
stdio.h file, 139
stdout file, 164
strcat() function, 136
strcmp() function, 95, 103–104, 110

strcpy() function, 51, 58, 105, 128, 136
strings, 46, 50–51
  converting digits to floating-point
    number, 80
  converting digits to integer, 79
  declaring size, 51
  pointers for processing, 138
  putting in file, 163–164
  with unknown length, 54
string constants, 50
strlen() function, 51
strncpy() function, 105, 107, 128
structures, 138, 143
subscripts, 182
summary, 118
summary() function, 122, 124, 126, 127,
    132, 134
switch, 90
switch statement, 180
switch-case statement, 42, 66
  break statement with, 39
  format, 35

tab character (\t), 49
test program, 17
  for Julian date conversion, 31–32
text editor, 16
tiny-c, 142
title, 117
title() function, 42, 44, 59–60
toupper() function, 66, 95
type conversions, with *sscanf()* function,
    77
typedef statements, 140, 143

Unix C, 121, 146
  procedure for using, 152–153
  program changes required by, 159–160
  redirecting I/O, 165
unsigned numbers, 68
usability, as feature of C compiler, 145–
    146
user's manual, with compiler, 145
utility functions, 157–158

variable types
  floating (*See* floating-point numbers)
  characters, 46–49
  global (*See* global variables)
  integer, 35
  multiple use of, 92

variables, 7
    declaration of, 24, 178
    expressing constants as, 125
    extracting from string with *sscanf()*, 76
    local, 66, 178
    rules for naming, 9
    scope, 67
variance, 167–169

week-day determination for date,
    program for, 35–38
while loop, 42, 66, 90
while statements, 39, 72, 179
    format, 38
    nested, 105
    relational operators in, 29

Whitesmith's, Ltd., C compiler from, 147, 148
Wilcoxon Rank test, 173, 174
WordStar, file conversion to ASCII text, 165–166
write() function, 144
writeout() function, in sort process, 108, 110, 111
writing to files, 82–83

Xenix C, 146
    procedure for using, 152–153
    program changes required by, 159–160
    redirecting I/O, 165

yjul() function, 27, 31